YOU'VE GOT IT, I WANT IT!

How Jealousy, Envy, and Coveting Disturb Our Hearts and Flavor Life

ENDORSEMENTS

One of the things I have always admired and enjoyed in Brenda Poinsett's writing is the authentic way that she addresses issues that all women struggle with. She does it in an honest, genuine and biblically based manner. *You've Got It, I Want It* is yet another example of her genuine writing style. All of us at some point have dealt with envy and jealousy. Through her insightful writing she gives biblical examples of how people in the Bible have dealt with similar feelings.

As you read through the chapters of the book you will find comfort and peace in learning to deal with these feelings. Her writing crosses all generations, whether young or more seasoned in your walk. It will help you to realize that we are all human and have similar struggles and it is ok to confess those feelings openly.

This book is a must read as an individual or used as a women's group study. The study questions at the end of each chapter will cause you to think and share your feelings about the contents. I pray this book will become a treasure to you as a believer or in your women's ministries group.

—**Vicki Smith**, Executive Director, General Baptist Women's Ministry

The raw honesty Brenda writes with will resonate with every female. She has brought to light the thoughts many

of us prefer to keep secret in the dark. Her boldness in calling out jealousy and envy for what it is, and how it damages our callings, makes the reader want to be bold in calling it out in their own lives. Women can be everything God has intended them to be, fully satisfied in his plans for them, and this book paves the way on how to come to that understanding. It's a must read!
—**Jayne Patton**, Speaker, Author, Founder of Altered Ministries

As a Pastoral Counselor and Advanced Christian Life Coach serving adult women, I see spiritual heartburn almost daily in my clients. I also recognize from working in mental health for over 25 years that we call the intestines "the long brain" because so many of our emotions are rooted and felt there. Jealously, envy and coveting keep women bound and unable to walk in the freedom Jesus paid for. I personally can't wait for this book to be published so that I can share it with my clients. I believe that they will see themselves in the words of these pages and benefit greatly from the questions at the end of each chapter. Brenda has done it again by being transparent and then providing thought provoking questions that will lead to honest answers. I highly recommend this book and the author.
—**Myla P. Erwin**, MA, CPC, Higher Level Life Coaching & Soul Care

On a personal level, *You've Got It, I Want It* speaks to my heart, and as the Women's Ministry Director at my church, I find the issue of jealousy and envy to be pretty common. I think many times though, we don't label or acknowledge these feelings, but rather ignore them. Brenda brings this unpleasant topic to the surface in such a way that grabs your attention and invites the reader to address these feelings with wisdom from God's Word.
—**Bobbie Jackson**, Women's Ministry Director at The Ridge

Brenda Poinsett explores what the Bible says about jealousy, envy and coveting to help women understand these emotions so they don't negatively affect our relationships with ourselves, with others and with God. Brenda expertly gives examples of biblical characters and personal experiences regarding these emotions. Brenda also shares how she has resolved some of these feelings in her own life.

—**Jan Turner**, President, Missouri Woman's Missionary Union

YOU'VE GOT IT, I WANT IT!

How Jealousy, Envy, and Coveting Disturb Our Hearts and Flavor Life

BRENDA POINSETT

COPYRIGHT

You've Got It, I Want It

Cover and Interior Design: Derinda Babcock
Editor(s): Mary Johnson, Deb Haggerty

PUBLISHED BY: Elk Lake Publishing, Inc., 35 Dogwood Drive, Plymouth, MA 02360, 2020

Library Cataloging Data

Names: Poinsett, Brenda. (Brenda Poinsett)
You've Got It, I Want It / Brenda Poinsett
176 p. 23cm x 15cm (9 in x 6 in.)
Identifiers: ISBN-13: 978-1-64949-385-9 (paperback) | 978-1-64949-386-6 (trade paperback) | 978-1-64949-387-3 (e-book)

Key Words: Taming Powerful Emotions; How to Have a Tranquil Heart; Being Content with Who I Am and What I Have; Why Do I Feel This Way?;Naming What You Feel; How to Have a Peaceful Heart and a Brighter Life; What the Bible Says About Jealousy and Envy

Library of Congress Control Number: 2021946965 Nonfiction

DEDICATION

To Barbara Phillips Watson,
who came along at the right time

Table of Contents

ACKNOWLEDGMENTS

Many thanks to what I consider "my team"—Bob Poinsett, Judith Mills, and Myrna Turner. They read every word of *You've Got It, I Want It*, made suggestions, found errors, and offered encouragement. I would welcome their input on any project I might attempt.

Thanks also to Barbara Phillips Watson, whose critiques sparked some serious considerations and conversations. Barbara caused me to think hard about some of the book's content, resulting in some manuscript changes. The book's content became clearer in some areas because of Barbara's input.

I appreciate the prayers and interest of friends and family members such as Jan Turner, Annette Huber, Margie Kruse, Mary Rose Fox, Sue Johnson, Alicia Ruff, Mona Mundwiller, Janet Hofer, Jim Poinsett, and Ben Poinsett. Ben gets a special thanks because he kept my computer up and running and solved all my technical issues.

Finally, I want to thank Deb Haggerty, Susan K. Stewart, Mary W. Johnson, Derinda Babcock, and everyone else at Elk Lake Publishing who worked hard to get this book out. One sentence in a comment Deb made in an internet group to which we belong prompted me to contact her. I like to believe it was God's timing. This belief has been reinforced as I've worked with Susan, Mary, and others to turn my manuscript into a book. It has been a pleasure to work with them.

I treasure all persons listed here for their interest and support. I trust the book is better because of their participation. I know I'm a better person because of their involvement in my life.

INTRODUCTION—A HEART DISTURBED

I never get jealous. Do you? Actually, it would be more accurate to say seldom. If the subject ever came up—and it hardly ever does—I'd say, "I can count on one hand the number of times I've been jealous."

How about envy? Now that's a word I've used, but only in a positive sense. When recognizing some special privilege another person was experiencing, I'd say something like, "What an opportunity! I envy you." If a friend were heading to a retreat in a scenic area, I'd say, "How nice for you! I envy you getting to go."

Both jealousy and envy involve *wanting* of some kind, something I didn't give much thought to. I was busy living life as a homemaker, an adjunct college instructor, and an active church member. There wasn't time to think about *wanting* what others had, and there didn't seem to be a reason to. I liked my life the way it was.

Imagine my annoyance then when fleeting moments of what I came to call pangs of jealousy started disturbing my peace. Oh, not in a drastic way. It was more like heartburn. You experience some discomfort, but you don't pay much attention when it occurs. You don't talk about it or analyze it. You swallow a couple of Tums and go on. That's how I reacted when thoughts like these started popping up.

- One of my nieces worked for a private college in a small, scenic Midwestern town. When she told me she was thinking about applying for a job in a large city, I thought, *I wouldn't move if I were her. I would love a situation like hers.*
- I was walking on the campus of the high school near where we lived when a teacher about my age exited the building. As I waved, I mumbled to myself, "She sure has it made—a good salary, competence and success in her field. Must feel really good."
- One of my students bubbled with enthusiasm as she told me about several job possibilities she was considering when she graduated. I smiled encouragingly, but to myself, I said, *I wish I had her options.*

Since these mental intrusions never lasted long, I never stopped and gave them consideration. I wasn't concerned. The feelings weren't causing much disturbance, just a brief discomfort at the time. When the intrusions increased in frequency, I became somewhat puzzled, but not enough to stop and give them notice. No harm was being done. I might have gone on that way and missed out on some valuable insight, if I hadn't thrown a magazine across the room.

The Flying Magazine

Home alone one evening, I snuggled deep into a comfortable chair. I started reading a magazine that had just arrived. Solitude, a fresh crisp magazine, and a comfy chair—my idea of luxury. I leisurely turned the pages, reading whatever appealed to me—such a nice change from what I read for teaching. My contentment was interrupted when I read about an author who had three book contracts on her desk. *Three contracts?! You've got to be kidding!*

In disgust, I threw the magazine across the room. I thought of some writer friends who would give anything to have one contract. I had written some books, and I knew how hard it was to get a book contract. *And this author has three! Unbelievable!*

I know, I know. You're thinking, *Brenda, throwing a magazine is no big deal.* You're right, it isn't. No one was hurt, no lamps were broken, and no one saw me. But the fact that it was an outward, tangible act caught my attention. I couldn't ignore it. I turned out the lights and sat thinking. Did this act have any connection with the pangs of jealousy I had been experiencing? Were my feelings trying to tell me something? If so, what?

I didn't get an answer that night, but I did get a raised consciousness. I started noticing references to jealousy and envy in the Bible as I taught courses in Bible Literature. It's like when you know you are going to become a parent, you start noticing how other parents handle their children. Or when you want to remodel your kitchen, you enter every kitchen with a keen awareness of your surroundings. All "systems" are on alert.

I was amazed at how often jealousy, envy, and coveting are mentioned in the Bible. If you look at jealousy and envy in the Bible, you will soon be looking at coveting too. The three are related. They all involve *wanting,* which can be good or bad.

Wanting opens our eyes to possibilities. It can alert us to things that might make our life better or easier or our work more efficient and productive. We see something in another person—a character trait, a particular skill or expertise—and *wanting* it propels us to act. We identify what we want and pursue it, something we might never do unless we wanted what someone else had.

You know the importance of wanting if you have a high school senior in your life as one of my friends currently does. She's exasperated with her son who doesn't know what he wants to do after graduation. When she asks him, he shrugs his shoulders and says, "I dunno." She *wants* him to *want* something! Wanting definitely has value, but the Bible is also clear that wanting has a darker, more troubling side.

The Darker Side

The Bible contains numerous examples of people who wanted something or someone so much that it led to relationship disturbances, emotional upheavals, violent acts, dishonesty, greed, selfishness, strife, ineffective leadership, and idolatry. Perhaps this is why the Bible is filled with so many warnings about jealousy, envy, and coveting. Warnings were included in God's instructions for living (the Law), in the preaching of the prophets, in Jesus's teachings, and in New Testament letters. It's as if God is alerting us to something about which we should all be aware. It's as if he is saying, "Wanting is something that will affect your relationship with me, with others, with your serving effectively, and with your enjoyment of life."

The sheer volume of biblical material on wanting made an impact. I realized I needed to stop and consider the feelings I was experiencing. If I didn't, the pangs of jealousy might take up permanent residence in my inner being and grow into something harmful and destructive. One verse in particular stood out to me. One of the Proverbs says, "A heart at peace gives life to the body, but envy rots the bones" (Proverbs 14:30 NIV).

I was—and still am—a woman who desires inner peace. I was also interested in "life to the body" as my life was changing. My youngest child was getting ready to leave for college. Frequently on my mind was the question: *What will I do with the rest of my life?* The landscape ahead looked bleak. I wanted a vibrant life filled with meaning and purpose. I didn't want envy, no matter how mild it appeared, to rot my "bones." That's why I decided to recognize what I was feeling, figure out why, and if necessary, make some changes in my life. This pursuit wasn't easy, but it was worthwhile.

The Pursuit

Studying emotions is never an easy study because emotions are hard to define and hard to understand. Casually, many of us use jealousy, envy, and coveting in different ways than English teachers define them. If you were taking an English test, here's what you would want to remember.

- Jealousy is something you feel about someone or something you already have and don't want to share or have taken away.
- Envy is what you feel towards someone who has something you want.
- Coveting is what you feel about the thing you want that someone else has.

And yet in our everyday world we don't often use the words this way. We interchange these words, and people seem to understand what we mean. They know wanting is disturbing our heart in some way.

Not only do we use these words differently, but their definitions have changed through the years. As I studied jealousy, envy, and coveting in the Bible, I had to work at understanding what the words meant then as well as what they mean today.

Complicating the study even further was the fact that jealousy, envy, and coveting have cousins—emotions that often reside along with them such as anger, resentment, depression, and malice. This makes them all the more powerful as peace disturbers, contributing to some really hard-to-treat cases of spiritual heartburn in the same way physical, unrelenting heartburn can indicate serious health problems.

Despite these difficulties, seeing what the Bible had to say about jealousy, envy, and coveting was a fascinating experience. Interesting people. Intriguing situations. I learned so much. For one thing, I had been jealous more times than I could count on one hand! But more importantly, I gained knowledge and grew spiritually in the process.

As I gained a better understanding of jealousy, envy and coveting, I realized our goal shouldn't be to eliminate them from our lives. How colorless our lives would be! Rather our goal should be to control them so they don't negatively affect our relationship with ourselves, with others, and with God.

I came to better understand people and their behavior. When I might have previously reacted to something with *You did what*?! I now find myself saying *So that explains it!* Their actions are motivated by jealousy, envy, or coveting. These emotions can hamper human bonding, interfere with friendships, break up families, affect dynamics at work and even interfere with fellowshipping and partnering with fellow believers.

Through my biblical study, I was able to gain the heart at peace I wanted. I also found the answer to my question about what I would do with the rest of my life. It didn't happen immediately, but "the word of God is alive and active" (Hebrews 4:12 NIV). It is "sharper than any double-edged sword, it penetrates even to dividing soul and spirit, joints and marrow; it judges the thoughts and attitudes of the heart" (Hebrews 4:12 NIV). As I studied, I certainly found my thoughts and attitudes being judged.

It took a while for this to happen because the roots of my pangs of jealousy were deep and intertwined with other emotions. My spiritual heartburn, which I originally thought wasn't anything to be concerned about, was a symptom of a deeper problem.

Through digging around inside, unwrapping emotions, and applying what I was learning, I discovered there was an issue affecting my relationship with God. A problem developed I hadn't identified, let alone allowed to surface. Nevertheless, it was there and was surfacing as fleeting sparks of jealousy. I don't know if I'd have made this discovery—and righted my relationship with God—if it hadn't been for a flying magazine prompting me to study the Bible. The discovery not only cured my heartburn but enhanced my life. I grew and gained in the process of studying what the Bible had to say about jealousy, envy, and coveting. That's why I want to share with you what I learned.

Do you have spiritual heartburn? Is your inner peace being disturbed with feelings you can't quite identify? Do those feelings seem to have something to do with *wanting* what others have? Do you want to name those feelings? Do you want to understand them and learn from them? Do you want to control them? Do you want to improve your relationships with others by better understanding them? Live in harmony with others without wishing you had what they had? Do you want to fully appreciate the person God created you to be? Does your relationship with him need improvement? If so, I invite you to look with me at the experiences of people in the Bible whose situations involved wanting. I don't know about you, but I seem to understand emotions better when I see how they work in other people's lives. I need examples. That's why this book is about biblical characters—people like you and me who at times in their lives dealt with wanting, its power, and its consequences.

We will also learn about ways we can deal with our feelings. While the Bible helps us understand emotions, it doesn't leave us bewildered. It offers us ways to grow so we can gain control of our emotions, be at peace with ourselves, and improve our relationships with others and with God.

At the end of each chapter are questions—questions we can ask ourselves or discuss with others. These questions stir our thinking and may even spur us to action. Who knows? Learning from these Bible characters may prompt as much growth in your life as it did in mine. If it does, you will be blessed, and your life will be enriched. You'll have a tranquil heart and a vibrant life.

CHAPTER 1—EVE: WHEN SEEING CREATES DESIRE

We're going to begin our study of what disturbs the heart by looking at Eve, the Bible's first woman. You might find this odd because the Bible doesn't describe her as being jealous, envious, or covetous. Besides, there wouldn't have been other people around except Adam to be jealous of or to envy. Neither would there have been a need to covet, since all Eve's needs were met in the environment God provided for her and Adam.

I'll admit Eve's experience is an unusual choice, but I include her story here because I've found wisdom for living in the early pages of Genesis. The creation account offers valuable truths about our nature and the world we live in—truths that haven't changed through the years. I believe Eve's experience in particular offers us insight about what we want and why we want it. Let's take a look at her story and see if you agree.

In the Garden

God provided Adam and Eve an environment, the Garden of Eden, where all their needs were met, and he gave them meaningful work to do. God only restricted them in one area. God told Adam, "You may eat the fruit of any tree in the garden, except the tree that gives knowledge of what is good and what is bad" (Genesis 2:17). They could eat the fruit of any other tree in the garden but not of this particular one. They had a choice to make—to eat or not eat the forbidden fruit. Satan, in the form of a serpent, appeared to "help" them with their choice.

The serpent said to Eve, "Did God really tell you not to eat fruit from any tree in the garden?" Satan exaggerated God's one limitation. He made it sound as if God were depriving Adam and Eve of *all* the fruit in the garden, as if he were asking too much of them.

To Eve's credit, she corrected the serpent. She said, "We may eat the fruit of any tree in the garden ... except the tree in the middle of it. God told us not to eat the fruit of that tree or even touch it; if we do, we will die" (Genesis 3:2–3). At this point, she interpreted God's restriction as God's protection. This was God's way of looking after her and Adam.

The serpent, however, persisted by trying to arouse envy in Eve. He said, "God said that because he knows when you eat it, you will be like him. You will know what is good and what is bad." In other words, "Don't you want to be like God, Eve? Don't you want to be superior to other creatures? Wouldn't you like to have exceptional knowledge?"

Eve had a crucial choice to make: eat the fruit as the serpent suggested, or obey God and not eat it. Eve deliberately chose not to obey God. She ate the fruit. What took her from defending God to disobeying him? It was what she *saw*.

When Eve "saw that the tree was good for food, and that it was pleasant to the eyes, and a tree to be desired to make one wise, she took of the fruit thereof, and did eat" (Genesis 3:6 KJV). When the Bible says "she *saw*," it wasn't like seeing a stop sign and choosing to come to a complete stop. It wasn't like seeing crumbs on the floor and getting a broom to sweep. This is *seeing* that stirred her thoughts and aroused her emotions. This *seeing* disturbed her soul.

What she *saw* created a desire in her so strong that she gave in. She ate the forbidden fruit. She wanted the fruit more than she wanted to obey God. That's the trouble with seeing. It can make us desire what we want more than what God wants.

This *seeing-wanting* connection shows up over and over in the Bible.

> When his [Joseph's] brothers *saw* that their father loved Joseph more than he loved them, they hated their brother so much that they would not speak to him in a friendly manner" (Genesis 37:4 author's italics).
>
> When I [Achan] *saw* among the spoils a goodly Babylonish garment, and two hundred shekels of silver, and a wedge of gold of fifty shekels weight, then I [Achan] *coveted* them, and *took* them. (Joshua 7:21, KJV, author's italics)
>
> One day, late in the afternoon, David got up from his nap and went to the palace roof. As he walked around up there, he *saw* a woman taking a bath in her house. She was very beautiful. So he sent ... messengers to get her; they brought her to him and he made love to her. (2 Samuel 11:2–4, author's italics)
>
> Simon *saw* that the Spirit had been given to the believers when the apostles placed their hands on them. So he offered money to Peter and John, and said, "Give this power to me too, so that anyone I place my hands on will receive the Holy Spirit." (Acts 8:18–19, author's italics)

What we *see* may prompt us to want something good or that would lead to a good outcome, so we would never want to be without Eve's eyes. But as her experience and the above examples show, we need to be aware of the *seeing-wanting* connection. It creates desires that ignite emotions such as jealousy, envy and coveting. Once these emotions invade the heart, their power is hard to resist, and we find it difficult not to act or react in some way. *I want it, so I'm going after it. She's got it, and it should be mine*. This is particularly true when we let what we see replay itself over and over in our minds. If we nourish and encourage desires long enough, the desires are more likely to become action. Stanley Jones, a twentieth-century Methodist missionary and theologian, put it this way: "Seeing creates desire and desire creates emotion, and in the battle between the emotion and the will, the emotion nearly always wins."[1]

That's why we need to be alert to what particularly appealed to Eve about the forbidden fruit. These are key areas of vulnerability.

1. *Sensual appeal.* Eve looked at the fruit and saw how good it would be to eat. It would taste so good! She imagined how full and satisfied she would feel. You could broaden this temptation to include any of the physical drives of the body such as hunger or sex. Think: How long could you look at a three-layered carrot cake or a chocolate sundae without eating it? What prompts a person to look at someone of the opposite sex and appraise his or her body? As Jesus said, "Anyone who *looks* at a woman and *wants* to possess her is guilty of committing adultery with her in his heart" (Matthew 5:28–29, author's italics).
2. *Aesthetic appeal.* The fruit had visual appeal. It called out to Eve, dazzling her with its beauty. Once alerted to this, I realized aesthetic appeal explained some of the heartburn I sometimes experience during the Christmas season. Each year, I decorate my home with ornaments, wreaths, and manger scenes I've collected through the years. I like doing this and find joy in the process. I stand back and admire the effect when I'm done; I am pleased, and then I go to a department store where the Christmas lights are bright and the decorations shiny. As I look at them, it doesn't take long before an inner voice starts saying, "I want it, I want it, I

want decorations like these." The dazzling effect of the store's decorations outshine my recycled home decorations so much that I am no longer content with what I have.

3. *Position appeal.* The fruit would make her wise, as wise as God. Oh, wow! Wouldn't that be a powerful position to have?! For us, this may mean seeing ourselves as having an edge over another person or persons, as in my house looks better than your house, my children are more well-behaved, I make more money than you do, or I'm more attractive. Here, as we see this happening in numerous situations, I'm going to refer to this effect as one-upmanship.

The apostle John warns us about these same three areas of vulnerability, only the three are expressed much more strongly, as if the understanding of their power had solidified through the years. John called them "the lust of the flesh, and the lust of the eyes, and the pride of life" (1 John 2:16 KJV).

Herschel H. Hobbs, a Baptist pastor who wrote and edited numerous books and commentaries, said, "every temptation falls within one of these categories."[2] I wouldn't go so far as to say every temptation, but many of them do. These are areas where we are vulnerable to the power of wanting—areas where Satan can work effectively and powerfully. We need to be aware of these areas so we will recognize temptation and not give in as Eve did, because there are consequences when we do.

Consequences

After Eve ate the forbidden fruit, she shared it with Adam. Without protesting, he also ate the fruit. It must have looked good to him, too!

Afterward, their lives changed, and not for the better.

They lost their luxurious environment, the Garden of Eden, where all their needs were met. Now they had to work hard and endure pain.

Adam and Eve viewed themselves differently. They felt shame and embarrassment. Instead of admitting what they had done and claiming responsibility, Adam blamed Eve, and Eve blamed the serpent. Their relationship with God changed too. They no longer felt comfortable in his presence. They hid from him when they heard God walking in the garden.

When our relationship with God is diminished, this change can be obvious to others, but often it is hidden. Something inside changes; something is different. Our connection with God encounters interference. Our heart is disturbed; we are no longer as comfortable as we once were or as we could be in his presence.

So what do you think? Is there evidence enough here to make you appreciate how *seeing* affects desire? There was for me, but I confess when my spiritual heartburn began, I could recognize this better in others than in myself. If I wanted relief, I was going to have to ask: What was I seeing in my niece, the experienced teacher, my students, and others that I wanted? Although I couldn't yet articulate what it was, I believed it was better than what I had, and that was enough to prompt feelings of jealousy and envy. The question now was what I was going to do about it.

Growth Questions (Genesis 3:1–19)

1. What did the serpent first ask Eve (3:1)? How was he trying to make her feel?
2. What did the serpent say to arouse envy in Eve (3:4)?
3. What three enticements motivated Eve to eat the forbidden fruit (3:6)?
4. How are the apostle John's descriptions of these three enticements (1 John 2:16) similar to Eve's? How are they different?
5. Which one of these three enticements gives you the most trouble?
6. How did Adam and Eve's relationship with God change after they ate the forbidden fruit (3:8)?
7. What three questions did God ask Adam and Eve after they ate the forbidden fruit (3:8,11,13)? How did Adam and Eve respond?
8. What images from television, advertisements, social media, etc. affect our desires? What do those images have in common with the three enticements Eve faced?

CHAPTER 2—CAIN: WHEN HE GOT IT, I WANTED IT

Perhaps it is the temptation to be like God, to be superior, that turns Eve's eyes into comparative eyes. Those eyes of hers we inherited always seem to be looking at others and measuring ourselves. This is not altogether a bad thing.

As we progress through life's various stages, we can evaluate our progress against that of others. *How am I doing? Am I where I ought to be at this time in life?* We can check our children's progress. *Her one-year-old is walking. Should my one-year-old?*

Comparison may result in motivation. As we notice how a fellow employee's hard work paid off with a promotion, we think, *Perhaps I need to work harder. If not, I may be in this position the rest of my life.*

But comparison can also be detrimental and make us miserable, which is what happened to Eve's son Cain. He measured himself against his brother, Abel. It wasn't a wise move. He didn't know trouble could come from seeing.

WHAT CAIN SAW

Cain and Abel were Adam and Eve's first two children. Abel was a shepherd, a keeper of flocks. Cain was a farmer who worked the soil. Both men made an offering to God. Cain offered some of his harvest. Abel, on the other hand, gave a first-born lamb from his fold. He killed the lamb and presented the best parts to God.

God was pleased with Abel's offering. He accepted his sacrifice, but he rejected Cain's, and Cain noticed. He compared God's response to Abel with God's response to him, and he didn't like what he saw. Some say Cain envied Abel. Others say he was jealous. I'm more prone to go with jealousy because Cain was deprived of what he thought and possibly assumed would be his.

The Bible describes Cain's reaction as anger. Daniel Goleman, in his book *Emotional Intelligence*, described jealousy as "a variant of anger that also melds sadness and fear."[1] I would imagine all these feelings were involved in Cain's experience. Jealousy because his brother bested him. Anger because it didn't seem fair. He made an offering, too. Sadness because God didn't approve of his sacrifice, and fear of what this might mean for his future. What a volatile mixture.

What Cain was experiencing was so strong, his feelings were evident in his face. His countenance changed; a scowl appeared. A facial reaction doesn't always happen with heart disturbers. Often secret feelings are hidden away where no one knows anything is bothering us. But Cain's change in appearance reminds us what we're experiencing on the inside may very well be evident on the outside. Your face may turn red. You may have a somber look, a furrowed brow, sagging shoulders or any number of other signs that indicate your misery. In Cain's case, his scowl was evidence of an internal volcano—one that could erupt at any moment, and it might have if God hadn't intervened.

"Then the Lord said to Cain, 'Why are you angry? Why that scowl on your face? If you had done the right thing, you would be smiling" (Genesis 4:6–7). These questions were not for God to enlighten himself. He knew why Cain was angry and why his countenance had changed. His questions were designed to lead Cain to acknowledge what he was feeling and why. We might follow a similar approach if we find ourselves livid when we compare ourselves with others. In situations like this, we can gain insight by asking questions such as these.

What am I feeling? God named what Cain was feeling: anger. When our feelings are mixed up and intertwined like they were in Cain's case, we may have to work at untying them, pulling them apart, and naming them. When we separate them, we can assess our feelings, and odd as it sounds, gain some control over them.

Why do I feel this way? Why couldn't Cain just acknowledge Abel got God's approval and go on his way? Was approval something he had been strongly aiming for? Or did the emotional response come in a flash as jealousy sometimes does?

While there has been much conjecture from scholars about the reason Cain's sacrifice was rejected and Abel's accepted, there is no indication in the biblical text as to the reason why. What the Bible is clear about, though, is Cain's reaction and God's response. He was furious, and God wanted to help him change his feelings. Asking ourselves why we feel the way we do can help us change.

What was I doing, or where was I? This question is not always necessary to ask ourselves but sometimes can give significant clues. Jealousy often is associated with a jealous lover, but the emotion can come in quieter ways and in places and for reasons we would never suspect. Cain's jealousy was born at the altar in a religious setting performing a religious act and wanting to please God. As odd as it sounds, our religious experiences may be cause for comparison.

We may notice God seems more pleased with someone else than with us, even though we are trying in our own ways to please him. When someone gets praise for their effort, which is not even close to what we've done, we are tempted to respond with jealousy and even anger.

Are others aware of what I am feeling? Have several people mentioned to you that you seem to be frowning a lot? Do they ask you what's wrong? Are you sharp or cross with others in your family or group? If these questions are valid, you may have a volcano brewing inside you, and you need to do something about it unless you want it to erupt and cause you even more problems.

Do I want to change? Jealousy and envy by their very nature can make you want to hold on to your feelings. You feel justified in how you have responded to comparing yourself with others. You rehearse your grievances over and over. But if you become weary of a heavy heart, perhaps you need to consider whether or not you want to change. If you do, God will help you.

God wanted to help Cain by getting him to acknowledge his feelings, confess what was in his heart, and accept responsibility for his actions. If he would, then God could help Cain. He could turn the scowl into a smile. If he would not, his emotional state could become a hotbed for growing sin. As these emotions take root and grow, they can morph into something destructive and damaging, which was what happened to Cain. God said to him, "[Sin] wants to rule you, but you must overcome it" (Genesis 4:7). Cain had a choice to make.

- If Cain chose to do well (see Genesis 4:7), then he would be lifted up. He would receive the approval he wanted. God would accept Cain and his worship if Cain repented, released the strong emotions swirling around inside him, and changed his attitude toward his brother. There was still time to gain God's approval.
- If Cain chose not to do well, sin would take advantage of his decision. Sin is always looking for weaknesses in an individual and trying to gain a foothold. If Cain continued to allow his hurt feelings to smolder, sin would grow to dominate his life.

God's message to Cain was both a warning and an encouragement. The way Cain was going, he was heading for worse troubles. God pointed out to him that he could stop the process. In essence, God was saying, "You can do this. You can master your feelings. You can change." Cain now had the opportunity to do something about his *wanting*. The choice was his.

What Cain Did

Instead of answering God's questions and taking his warning seriously, Cain invited Abel to go with him to the fields. It was a casual invitation—kind of like what we might say to a sibling: "Let's go see how the corn is growing." Abel suspected nothing.

Abel, trusting his brother, went with Cain. Abel had no idea of what fate awaited him, but Cain knew. His mental wheels were turning as they walked together. If he could get Abel away from human habitation, he would get rid of Abel. And that's exactly what happened. When they arrived in the fields, Cain killed his brother.

Cain's act made no sense. He did not get what he wanted. While he might have been able to physically overpower his brother, the action did not make him superior to Abel. His ugly deed did not gain him God's approval and blessing. Killing Abel did not get him what he wanted, but fortunately the act did not get him beyond God's mercy. Instead of writing him off, God helped Cain once again. He held him accountable for his actions, but he was also merciful.

What God Did

God confronted Cain. He "asked Cain, 'Where is your brother Abel?'" (Genesis 4:9). Again, the question was not for God's enlightenment. God knew where Abel was. What he was doing was offering Cain an opportunity to confess, to say, "I have sinned." Instead, Cain answered, "I don't know," which was a lie. Cain knew exactly where Abel's dead body was. Cain hoped that by lying he could escape the consequences of his actions. Instead, he acted as if he had no responsibility for his brother. Cain cynically said, "Am I supposed to take care of my brother?" (4:9). Sin was mastering him.

With that response, God became more direct. He said to Cain, "Why have you done this terrible thing? Your brother's blood is crying out to me from the ground, like a voice calling for revenge. You are placed under a curse and can no longer farm the soil. It has soaked up your brother's blood as if it had opened its mouth to receive it when you killed him. If you try to grow crops, the soil will not produce anything: you will be a homeless wanderer on the earth" (Genesis 4:10–12).

Cain couldn't believe what he was hearing! He was filled with fear. He "said to the Lord, 'This punishment is too hard for me to bear. You are driving me off the land and away from your presence. I will be a homeless wanderer on the earth, and anyone who finds me will kill me'" (Genesis 4:13–14).

Interesting, isn't it? Cain, who had no mercy for Abel, wanted mercy. And God, true to his nature, was merciful. He put a mark on Cain to warn anyone who met him not to kill him. The mark was designed to protect him from being slain by others. If anyone ignored the mark and killed Cain, seven lives would be taken in revenge. With that reassurance, Cain "went away from the Lord's presence and lived in a land called 'Wandering'" (Genesis 4:16). Cain ended up exiled, unable to experience God the way he once had and unable to be the person he once was.

This is a chance we take when we refuse to recognize strong feelings resulting from comparing ourselves and our situations with those of others. Failure to acknowledge our feelings can mess up our lives just as that failure did Cain's. I didn't want to take that chance. I wasn't worried about committing a violent crime as Cain did. Throwing a magazine is as violent as I get when upset.

I didn't want to be a restless wanderer, though. I wanted to lead a purposeful existence, looking neither to persons on my left or on my right as having more stimulating lives. I had a choice to make just as Cain did: acknowledge my feelings or ignore them.

Begrudgingly, I decided to acknowledge my feelings. I say begrudgingly because I didn't want to do the work of figuring out what I was feeling; I didn't want to answer the questions or make changes. I was clumping my feelings together, calling them "pangs of jealousy," although my English teacher friend said I was envious. Either way, a tinge of anger was sometimes attached to a pang. I didn't want to take the time to sort all these emotions out, because the work usually does take time.

Neither did I want to make any changes in my life. If I figured out what was behind my pangs of jealousy, I might need to make changes. I might have to repent and modify my behavior, which is seldom easy. But those words "sin is crouching at your door" haunted me (Genesis 4:7). If I didn't acknowledge my "pangs of jealousy," could they morph into a bigger problem? Affect my relationships? And most worrisome of all, continue to disturb my heart? I didn't want that to happen, so I continued my pursuit of what the Bible had to say about jealousy, envy, and coveting. Somewhere in there, I believed, was the help I needed to have a peaceful heart and a meaningful life. I believe there are answers for you, too. Sin wants to rule us, but with God's help, we can keep sin from mastering us.

QUESTIONS FOR GROWTH (GENESIS 4:1–16):

1. Would you label Cain's reaction to God's approval of Abel's offering as jealousy or envy? What other emotions were involved in Cain's reaction?
2. Who was Cain angry with? God? Abel? Himself?
3. How might a person's inner discontent be revealed outwardly?
4. What counsel did God give Cain regarding his future? What did Cain choose? Was his choice rational or irrational? Why is making a rational choice hard when you are jealous or envious?
5. Sin wanted to master Cain. What does "mastering" mean?
6. Did Cain's choice and subsequent actions get him what he wanted?
7. When God confronted Cain about his actions, what was Cain's reply? What did his reply indicate about his attitude?
8. How did God punish Cain after he murdered his brother (4:10–12)? Which part of Cain's punishment do you think was the hardest to bear?
9. How did God show grace to Cain even as he punished him (4:15)? What does this say to us about how God responds when we sin?

CHAPTER 3—SARAH: WHEN WISDOM IS NEEDED

Maybe you've had the experience of getting a child just what he wanted for Christmas. You saved for weeks and relished the thought of how he would react when he opened your gift. But that's not what happened. He looked at the item briefly and put it aside. You asked, "What's wrong?" He said, "It's not what I wanted."

Or perhaps you dated someone you just knew was going to be "the one." You went out with him for a few weeks and then started making excuses when he suggested what you two could do. He no longer held your interest. You had changed your mind.

Your new pastor was electric, a dynamo, boosting attendance from his very first Sunday. As the months passed, he often said, "You can always count on me to be here. I'm not going anywhere," and then one Sunday morning after being in the pulpit for ten months, he said, "God has called me to another church." You couldn't understand how he could change his mind so fast.

In this book we're considering the power of *wanting*: its attraction, its characteristics, its influence, and its consequences. From the above examples, you can see wanting gets complicated. We may change our mind about what we want. This may have been what happened to Sarah, Abraham's wife.

What She Wanted

In Sarah's (first known as Sarai) time, if you were female, you grew up anticipating being a mother. It was the natural thing to do. In her case, the cultural expectation of having children was strengthened because God had said to her husband Abram, "I will give you many descendants, and they will become a great nation ... through you I will bless all the nations" (Genesis 12:2–3). While this promise meant many things, it sealed for Sarai the expectation that she would have a child. After all, how could there be many descendants if there wasn't at least one child?

But a baby for Sarai didn't happen at the expected time in a woman's life. Years passed, and still no child. When it looked hopeless that she would ever conceive, she got an idea. Her slave girl, Hagar, could help. She said to Abram, "The Lord has kept me from having children. Why don't you sleep with my slave? Perhaps she can have a child for me" (Genesis 16:2). As startling as her proposal might sound, it was not an unusual practice in that part of the world then.

Giving Hagar to Abram must have been hard for Sarai. She was admitting to the possibility of never conceiving a child, and at the same time, encouraging her husband to sleep with another woman. (And, of course, this must have been hard for Hagar too. As a servant, she didn't have a choice about what was happening.) Yet in Sarai's thinking, her plan would give her the child she wanted and increase the possibility of Abram having many descendants. She would be able to experience motherhood and possibly have more children. If Hagar had more children, they would be considered Sarai's children.

Sarai's plan worked. Abram and Hagar conceived a child, and Ishmael was born. Now Sarai had a child to love and to care for, and she and Abram could count on God's plan for a people to be fulfilled.

God, though, didn't need Sarai's help. God meant what he said when he promised Abram he would have many descendants. While it was too late in Sarai's view, it was never too late from God's perspective. When Abram was ninety years old, God reaffirmed his plans for Abram and Sarai. He gave them new names in the process: Abraham and Sarah. Eventually, even after Sarah laughed at the possibility of ever giving birth, baby Isaac was born to Sarah and Abraham. At the time, she was around ninety years old, and Abraham was a hundred.

Sarah said, "God has brought me joy and laughter ... I have borne him [Abraham] a son in his old age" (Genesis 21:6–7). What a blessed time for this family. It looks like we could now end this family's story with "they lived happily ever after." Perhaps we could, if Sarah hadn't taken time to watch her children play.

A Heart Disturbed

When little Isaac was around two years old, it was time for him to be weaned. This called for a celebration, so "Abraham gave a great feast" (Genesis 21:8). During the festivities, the two sons played together. Ishmael was probably around thirteen years old at the time. Sarah stood by watching the boys play. Perhaps she wanted to make sure Ishmael wasn't too hard on little Isaac.[1] As the mother of three sons, I can understand why. Their playing can get a little rough.

As she watched, this could have been a special time of looking back and marveling at all that had transpired. She could have rejoiced in getting to be the mother of not one but two sons, when for a long time she thought she wasn't going to have children. But that's not what happened. Instead, her thoughts turned to the future, and to what she and Abraham would be leaving behind when they died. They didn't have many years left. She thought about Abraham's wealth and who would inherit it. She realized his wealth would be divided between his two sons. That meant Ishmael would get part of Abraham's wealth. He was Abraham's son just as Isaac was. She couldn't bear the thought.

She wanted Isaac to have the wealth—all the wealth. He was her flesh and blood—the child she and Abraham had created together. He should get *all* of Abraham's wealth. Ishmael should receive nothing. Even though she had once claimed Ishmael as her child—even though his very existence was her idea—she wanted to dismiss any rights Ishmael might have to Abraham's riches. She wanted everything for Isaac.

Had Sarah been thinking for some time about inheritance and the boys? Had she been calculating who would get what and how much? Did she come to the conclusion Ishmael shouldn't inherit any of their wealth? If she did, perhaps these thoughts resurfaced and strengthened as she watched her sons play.

Or did she experience a phenomenon known as the jealous flash—a sudden painful, disturbing pang of jealousy. This sharp feeling of jealousy can pop up at any time. It can be a good thing, such as raising a person's awareness about a situation that needs addressing. For example, someone is flirting with your spouse or boyfriend and, you need to be alert. But it can be a bad thing if you react too quickly or overreact. This is hard not to do, because a jealous flash often comes with a sense of urgency. You feel like you have to act and act *now*. You don't have to, but that's what it feels like, and the pang can be hard to ignore. What may happen then is you end up acting hastily and unwisely, which might be what happened to Sarah.

Sarah was so riled by the possibility of Ishmael's getting some of Abraham's inheritance that she acted immediately and forcefully. She said to Abraham, "Send this slave and her son away. The son of this woman must not get any part of your wealth, which my son Isaac should inherit" (Genesis 21:10). Now Sarah sees Ishmael as "her son," meaning Hagar's son, not "my son." She doesn't refer to Hagar by name but references her as "this woman." She didn't want the slave girl who had served her for a long time around any longer. Neither did she want the son who was the result of her planning. What she once wanted, she no longer wanted. I wince as I write that sentence. I know many women hold Sarah in high esteem, but I struggle with this part of her life. To want a child and then to not want the same child is hard for me to understand and to accept. I remember years ago a friend calling me, telling me about a writer's conference she had attended. She came home from the conference excited about what she learned and what it meant for her future. She said, "The trouble is, my children take up so much of my time. You know, if I didn't have children, I could be a successful writer."

I wanted to scream into the phone, "But you prayed for those children. You were barren and you prayed fervently. God responded and helped you adopt two children. Now you wish they weren't around so you could be a successful writer?!"

I was greatly distressed by this conversation, just as I was distressed by Sarah's changing her mind about Ishmael and how she treated Hagar and Ishmael.

Sarah wanted Ishmael far away where he could not get any part of Abraham's wealth. She had no concern for the welfare of Hagar and Ishmael—where they would go or how they would provide for themselves. She acted, and she acted quickly. She said to Abraham, "Send them away!"

Abraham was troubled, too, by Sarah's instructions "because Ishmael also was his son" (Genesis 21:11). He was bothered by what Sarah was telling him to do, but God reassured him the situation would work itself out. He let Abraham know Isaac's descendants would be the ones who would form the people chosen to represent him. God also affirmed that Ishmael was Abraham's son, too, and he would head a nation of people. They would be Ishmaelites.

Realistically, there were probably too many volatile emotions between Sarah and Hagar for them to continue to live together. Their relationship had had challenges even before this incident, and now with Sarah's antagonism toward Ishmael, separation was probably best, but she could have been merciful and seen that they were provided for. Instead Hagar and Ishmael had to leave and forage for themselves in the wilderness because they were sent away without anything. How unfair and insensitive of Sarah to have treated a mother and a boy this way—especially two who had contributed to her life the way they had.

Fortunately, when Hagar was moved to tears over their dreadful situation in the wilderness, God provided for them. That they survived doesn't make Sarah's actions appropriate. Her reaction to jealousy—whether it was calculated or came in a flash—was unreasonable, drastic, and inconsiderate. How it might have been different if she had exercised some wisdom.

Sarah didn't stop to think about a reasonable solution, a solution that might provide for Hagar and Ishmael and still be generous to Isaac. Neither did she go to Abraham and say, "We need to talk. I'm concerned about your legacy. Have you thought about how your wealth is going to be divided when you die?" Perhaps the two of them could have solved the inheritance problem together and worked out something that considered the needs of Hagar and Ishmael.

When Wisdom Is Needed

Sometimes when we're dealing with jealousy, trying to determine what's the best thing to do, it helps to ask ourselves questions such as these:

What is my jealousy urging me to do?

What options do I have?

If I follow through on any of these options, what will the end result be?

If I act, will I be better off or worse off?

Would anyone else be hurt by my actions?

What's the kind thing to do?

While this looks simple on paper, it is not. Being rational is hard when you are having strong, makes-you-want-to-act-immediately feelings of jealousy. This is why looking at the experiences of biblical characters who experienced feelings of jealousy, envy, and coveting is so important. We will become wiser in the process. We will be able to recognize these feelings in ourselves and often in others. We will learn how to control our feelings—what will work for us to not act irrationally. We will learn to hesitate when a flash of jealousy occurs, or stop long enough to let the flash's inherent energy wind itself down.

To see how Sarah and others changed their minds about what they once wanted doesn't mean we should never change our mind about what we want. This too takes wisdom to know when it's all right to change and when we need to stay the course. That mother who prayed for children and yet wished she didn't have them, in my opinion, needed to stay the course. The woman who changed her mind about the person she wanted to marry was probably right to do so. We can't know another person and see if we are compatible unless there is interaction. These kinds of situations are complicated. That's why we need wisdom, to be able to sort things and act appropriately with regard to ourselves and to others.

We can't keep flashes of jealousy from occurring in our lives, but we can keep them from contributing to spiritual heartburn or causing us to do something that hurts others. We can pause, identify our feelings, consider out options, and ask God to help us act wisely. And if we do, God will answer because God gives wisdom "generously and graciously to all" (James 1:5).

Questions for Growth (Genesis 21:1–14):

1. Could a possible root of Sarah's jealousy be having a need for a surrogate in the first place? Or was her jealousy something any mother might feel?
2. How does Sarah's experience compare with Cain's?
3. What kind of jealous flashes might a parent experience? Over what kinds of things? What might they want to protect in their children?
4. What kind of jealous flashes might a college student experience?
5. What kind of jealous flashes might a spouse experience?
6. How can Sarah's flash of jealousy help us understand the behavior of others?
7. Did age have anything to do with Sarah's jealousy? Was her feeling something an older person would experience? Would a younger person react in the same way?
8. When might a jealous flash serve a good purpose?
9. Once, before Ishmael was born, Sarah had sent the pregnant Hagar away because she had become proud and arrogant toward her. Abraham had no reaction at the time. This time he was upset when Sarah told him to send Hagar and Ishmael away. What might explain the difference?

CHAPTER 4—JOSEPH'S BROTHERS: WHEN THE HEART CAN'T FORGET

One of the most loved and inspirational stories in the Bible is Joseph's story. This son of Jacob suffered all kinds of hardships and unfair treatment including being sold by his brothers to slave traders, being falsely accused, and being put in prison. Yet he ended up in a position where he saved God's people from annihilation. We often take heart from his story—as we should—because we are reassured God can use for good whatever difficulties we might experience.

But for those of us interested in understanding jealousy, envy, and coveting, we might also want to look at his brothers' stories. They are not as inspiring, but they are insightful. From their experience, we can gain perspective on how these emotions sprout, grow, gain power, influence our behavior, and even disturb our hearts for a long, long time.

Many families are beset with tensions and conflicts that sometimes lead siblings to be jealous or envious of each other. Actually, it's pretty normal. The only way to guarantee sibling jealousy doesn't occur is to have one child. Jacob had twelve sons, and trouble started when he favored one over the others.

He sometimes kept Joseph home while his brothers were away working, taking care of the family's sheep and goats. He had a special coat made for Joseph but not for the other sons. When the brothers "*saw* that their father loved Joseph more than he loved them, they *hated* their brother so much that they would not speak to him in a friendly manner" (Genesis 37:4, author's emphasis).

Joseph fueled their dislike. When he did help his brothers care for the family's sheep and goats, he "brought bad reports to his father about what his brothers were doing" (Genesis 37:2b). Now that kind of behavior will not put you in good stead with your siblings. No one likes a tattletale.

Joseph also spoke of dreams he had—dreams that put him in a superior position. In one dream, he said, "We were all in the field tying up sheaves of wheat, when my sheaf got up and stood up straight. Yours formed a circle around mine and bowed down to it'" (Genesis 37:7). To the brothers, this meant Joseph saw himself as a king who would rule over them "so they hated him even more" (37:8).

Joseph was either obtuse or else he didn't care how his brothers felt, because he told them another dream. He said, "I saw the sun, the moon, and eleven stars bowing down to me" (Genesis 37:9). You didn't have to be very smart to figure out he meant their father, Jacob, Jacob's wife, and his brothers.

Consequently, "Joseph's brothers were jealous of him" (Genesis 37:11, see also Acts 7:9).[1] Their jealousy was so strong they determined they would do something about their irritating brother. The opportunity came one day when Jacob sent Joseph to the field to check on his brothers. When the brothers saw him coming, "they said to one another, "Here comes that dreamer. Come on now, let's kill him and throw his body into one of the dry wells" (37:19–20).

Fortunately, two brothers intervened. Reuben urgently tried to get his brothers not to kill Joseph. Instead, he suggested they throw him in a well. An even better idea occurred to Judah when he saw a caravan of Midianite [also called Ishmaelite] slave traders passing by on their way to Egypt. He said, "Let's sell him to these Ishmaelites"

(Genesis 37:27) so they did, which presented them with a problem. How would they explain Joseph's disappearance to their father?

They took Joseph's coat, dipped it in blood, and showed it to Jacob. The bloody coat convinced Jacob some wild animal had killed Joseph. "Jacob tore his clothes in sorrow and put on sackcloth" (Genesis 37:34) and "refused to be comforted" (37:35).

While the brothers tried to comfort their father, they were at the same time relieved. They would never have to listen to Joseph's stories of superiority again or see their father favor him. Their problems were solved! They could forget about Joseph, their jealousy, their hatred, and what they had done to him. Something happened to them twenty years later that shows otherwise.

A Family in Need

A famine occurred in Canaan where Jacob's family lived, and as their food supply dwindled, Jacob sent Joseph's ten half-brothers to Egypt, where he'd heard they had grain. He kept Benjamin, Joseph's younger full brother home with him. Unbeknownst to Jacob's family, Joseph was alive and well. While he had indeed been sold by the slave traders, he had risen in prominence in Egypt. Serving as their governor, he had the Egyptians to store up grain to be famine-ready. Now that the famine was occurring, Joseph was in charge of distributing the grain.

When the brothers arrived in Egypt and appeared before Joseph, they did not recognize him; however, he recognized them. Joseph asked them questions about their family, and then he insisted they go get Benjamin and bring him to Egypt if they wanted food.

The brothers couldn't believe this. How awful this would be for their father to even consider. They knew Jacob might not even let them return with Benjamin. That would mean no grain. With no grain, the family might starve! They said to each other, "Now we are suffering the consequences of what we did to our brother ... That is why we are in this trouble now'" (Genesis 42:21).

Reuben said, "I told you not to harm the boy, but you wouldn't listen. And now we are being paid back for his death" (Genesis 42:22). The heart remembered. The hatred, the jealousy, and the guilt were all there, taking up residence, and disturbing the heart.

But if they didn't go back, if they didn't face Jacob and return to Egypt with Benjamin, their whole family might starve to death, so they told Joseph they would go get their brother and bring him to Egypt.

Joseph then sold them grain. He kept one of the brothers behind to make sure they would come back with Benjamin in tow. He also had the money they paid for the grain put in their sacks. The brothers found the money on their way back home. "Their hearts sank, and in fear they asked one another, 'What has God done to us?'" (Genesis 42:28). Now they were really disturbed.

Jacob didn't like the idea just as the brothers thought, but as their situation grew more desperate, he allowed Benjamin to return to Egypt with their brothers. Once there, Joseph told them who he was in a deeply moving scene. In his remarks, he said, "God sent me ahead of you to rescue you in this amazing way and to make sure that you and your descendants survive. So it was not really you who sent me here, but God" (Genesis 45:7–8).

These are the words of a man who is not resentful or seeking revenge, whose heart isn't disturbed. He tells them to go get their father and bring him to Egypt. Get the whole clan!

When Jacob and the others arrived in Egypt, Joseph saw to it that they had food to eat and a place to live. You'd think that it would be obvious to the brothers that they were forgiven and they could quit being haunted by their past, but it didn't. In fact, their heartburn increased as fear was added to the mix.

As they took care of their flocks, as they migrated from pasture to pasture, the heaviness of their hearts pressed against their ribs. They couldn't let their guilt surface and deal with their hidden emotions because their father might find out how they had treated Joseph and deceived him. While Joseph appeared to forgive them, they just weren't sure. After their father died, they decided to approach him. Not that their motive was noble. Rather they were suspicious. Perhaps Joseph had been waiting for this moment—waiting for the father to not be around so he could repay them for the evil he had suffered at their hands. Even though Joseph had been loving, forgiving and kind, they were terrified of what he might do, so they sent a message to Joseph. They didn't go themselves, and they made their inquiry sound like it was their father's idea.

The message said, "Before our father died, he told us to ask you, 'Please forgive the crime your brothers committed when they wronged you.' Now please forgive us the wrong that we, the servants of your father's God, have done.'" (Genesis 50:16–17).

"Joseph said to them, 'Don't be afraid; I can't put myself in the place of God. You plotted evil against me, but God turned it into good, in order to preserve the lives of many people who are alive today because of what happened. You have nothing to fear. I will take care of you and your children.' So he reassured them with kind words that touched their hearts" (Genesis 50:19–21).

This is something they should have done earlier. If they had, they might have spared themselves years of inner turmoil. While they might have been unnerved at the prospect of approaching Joseph, passing the message off as their father's idea, it was the right thing to do. And we can learn from what they did.

They acknowledged the situation. Their father's death prompted them to admit their wrongdoing. What their hearts had remembered all through the years surfaced.

We can have feelings floating around inside, disturbing our hearts, and never acknowledge their presence in the sense of naming the feelings. Sometimes just realizing the way we are reacting to things today is because of what we experienced in childhood may be freeing. *So that explains it. That's why I have been reacting the way I have.*

When I mentioned sibling rivalry as a possible cause for adult jealousy over lunch at a retreat, Libby said, "There was a time when I would have laughed at your suggestion, but last year my husband started a new job that required many lunch meetings, often with only female coworkers. When he would tell me about their conversations, I seethed inside. I reminded myself how trustworthy Dan was, but still the lunches bothered me. One day I asked myself, *now why am I jealous*? Dan's a charming person, and when I thought about other women enjoying his company, I realized I wanted all his attention. I was one of four daughters, and I always had to vie for my father's attention. I didn't want to share Dan too. Interestingly, this insight helped me to calm down and accept the lunches as a legitimate part of my husband's work."

They took action. For Libby, just figuring out why she was jealous was enough to dispel her feelings, but for others action may be needed, especially when another person or persons are involved. Joseph's brothers couldn't read his mind. From our view, we could see he was not angry at them. He took in the whole family, he fed them, and he gave them a place to live. That doesn't sound like revenge, does it? But it didn't convince the brothers. Their misery had been around a long time, but finally with the sending of the message they were determined to find out once and for all. They took action. They went to the person who could give them the answer. Whatever conclusions we come to about persons we are jealous of, we might want to seek some verification. We may just discover as Joseph's brothers did that we are wrong in our estimate of the situation.

They asked for forgiveness. In their message to Joseph, the brothers said, "Please forgive the crime your brothers committed" (Genesis 50:17). If you concluded one of your siblings was getting preferential treatment at home, you might have been so upset you talked about them to others. As you did, out of your fury, you might have exaggerated what was done, said things that weren't really true. Or you might have wished calamity would befall them. (*Serves them right!*) To be free, to clear your heart, you may need to talk with them and seek their forgiveness. You might want to say something like this: "I'm sorry I've been angry at you. I was jealous, and I complained about you to others from time to time. I don't want to do that anymore. I want to right our relationship. Will you please forgive me?"

They allowed for the possibility God might work in their situation. Joseph had long ago (exactly when, we don't know) made peace with what happened because he saw God working for good in and through all his hardships. And God had. A people, a chosen people, had been saved to fulfill their destiny. They would have starved to death if Joseph hadn't ended up in Egypt where they could be fed and housed when the famine came. And he said as much to the brothers, "God turned it into good" (Genesis 50:20). Perhaps the brothers' hearts were warming to Joseph's vision and gaining a new perspective. In their message to Joseph, they referred to themselves as servants of his father's God. They were exercising faith. They were coming to the same conclusion as Joseph.

Perspective matters, which is why we too might want to believe God can bring something good out of our situation when we hold on to heart-disturbing emotions. The residue—the effect—of jealousy can be resolved. Relationships can be improved and restored, including our relationship with God. For this to happen, we must be willing to acknowledge our feelings, take action, ask forgiveness, and allow for the possibility that God can work for good in our situation. This story within a story doesn't tell us everything we need to know about jealousy, envy and coveting—we have so much more to learn. The story of Joseph's brothers, though, does reassure us that long-term feelings can be resolved. Our hearts don't have to be disturbed forever; we can find peace.

QUESTIONS FOR GROWTH (GENESIS 37:2–36, 50:15–21):

1. Why do you think Joseph revealed his dreams to his brothers? What did he hope to gain, or what did he expect to happen by doing this?
2. Growing up, how well did you get along with your siblings? Did your relationship with them change as you grew older?
3. What can we learn from Jacob and Joseph's story that would help us to be better parents?
4. The Bible says, "Jacob loved Joseph more than all his other sons, because he had been born to him when he was old" (Genesis 37:3). What is there about being old that would cause a parent to favor a particular child?
5. How does unequal treatment by a parent contribute to jealousy or envy within a child?
6. How long can a person carry a rage or bitterness against a sibling?
7. What can we learn from Joseph's experience with his siblings that will help us in our relationships with our siblings?
8. What can parents do to help their children love each other?
9. How might the brothers have better handled their jealousy than by selling Joseph to a group of slave traders?
10. Jacob is the one person who could have made a difference in this situation, but he did nothing but continued "thinking about the whole matter" (Genesis 37:11). Why do you think he didn't do anything? What are some things he could have done?
11. Can jealousy or envy among siblings ever be fully eliminated?

CHAPTER 5—MIRIAM AND AARON: WHEN PRAISE IS MISSING

When I was growing up, I saw my mother work very hard with little appreciation from others, particularly my father. She kept our house clean, worked a job, looked after five children, was active in church, was a good neighbor and was attentive to my father's needs. She even kept his shoes polished. While my father had many good qualities, offering praise was not one of them. As I observed my mother being so diligent without her work being acknowledged, I determined to marry someone who was appreciative. When I met Bob, he was so gracious, so forthcoming with affirming words, I thought, "Now this is a man I could scrub floors for!"

Let's face it. We all benefit when someone appreciates what we do. It's not that we are doing it to get compliments and praise. When we take on a role, we will do what that role calls for. If my husband never gave me another compliment, I would still do my best to fulfill my role. I committed myself to do that and I love him. When we respond to God's call to serve him, we don't say, "Okay, I will, if you see that I get recognition and praise for my service." Instead, we sing, "Give of your best to the Master," and do what he asks us to do. In doing either of these two things—or in committing to something else—we can get tired or discouraged. We can be tempted to get off-track if we go for a long stretch without some positive feedback. Our spirits languish. We are not as energized. While you are in a stretch like this, what if other people in a similar situation get praised and you don't? You may be tempted to think: How come people compliment her and never me? How come he gets a raise and a promotion and I'm overlooked? Why does she get noticed for her leadership ability and no one says a word about my organizational skills?

Moses's siblings Miriam and Aaron may have found themselves in a situation like this. The three of them were in the process of leading the Israelites toward the Promised Land. Somewhere along the way—and I can't pinpoint exactly where—Miriam and Aaron realized Moses was being praised, and they weren't. They became envious of Moses.

This feeling surfaced first as criticism. Miriam and Aaron criticized Moses for marrying "a Cushite woman" (Numbers 12:1). She might have been a woman from Ethiopia or from somewhere in Arabia. Either way, she was an "outsider" to Miriam and Aaron. Maybe, they thought he should have married someone who looked like them or who shared their beliefs and heritage. But that wasn't their real concern. Behind the criticism, something else was brewing. "They said, 'Has the Lord spoken only through Moses? Hasn't he also spoken through us?'" (Numbers 12:2).

Miriam and Aaron were proficient speakers. Aaron was Moses's spokesperson. When God called Moses, Moses insisted he could not face Pharaoh or deal with the Israelites because he was—in his estimation—"a poor speaker" (Exodus 4:10). Aaron, on the other hand, could speak well, so God called him to speak for Moses.

Miriam was a prophetess, meaning she proclaimed God's will and purpose. She also spoke through music. She led the Israelites in praising the Lord following the dramatic Red Sea experience, when they escaped the Egyptians who were in hot pursuit.

In their estimation, their words were just as important as Moses's. Therefore, they felt they should have been ranked equally with Moses. He was getting credit, and they weren't.

Moses didn't defend himself, and he didn't argue. It wasn't his nature to do so. He "was a humble man, more humble than anyone else on earth" (Numbers 12:3).

God, though, challenged Miriam and Aaron. He interrupted their conversation. He said, "Come out ye three unto the tabernacle" (Numbers 12:4 KJV). He appeared to them there in a cloud. He asked Aaron and Miriam to step forward where he talked directly to them. He sternly reminded them there were different callings and different ways of communicating.

God called Moses to be the leader of the Israelites, to gain their freedom, develop them as a people, and get them to the Promised Land. As God put it, he "entrusted" Moses "with all my [his] house" (Numbers 12:7 NRSV). To do this, Moses needed to be able to inquire of God at any time and receive a reply. They had to be in *constant* communication. God called Miriam and Aaron to be Moses's assistants. Miriam and Aaron were instruments with a particular function, through whom God made known his counsel and will *at times* to help with the leadership and development of the people.

God spoke directly: "mouth to mouth" (KJV) or "face to face" (Numbers 12:8 NRSV, NIV) with Moses. They had a particular kind of clear connection. With Miriam and Aaron, the communication wasn't as clear. He spoke at particular times to them in visions and dreams, a fuzzier type of communication.

His anger "burned against them" as he spoke (Numbers 12:9 NIV). When God finished, he departed immediately almost as if he were saying, "I don't have time for this. Why are you contrasting yourselves with someone who has a different role and purpose? Why don't you be you and let Moses be Moses? Why don't you fully explore and appreciate the roles I've given you instead of criticizing Moses?"

As he left, the cloud lifted, and there stood Miriam covered with leprosy. Aaron was left untouched even though they had both criticized and envied Moses. Now here's where I would have been jealous if I'd been Miriam. This doesn't seem fair to me. Does it to you?

Maybe Miriam was punished and Aaron wasn't because Miriam might have been the leader in their disgruntlement. Her name is given first in the biblical account (see Numbers 12:1) of this incident, even though when Miriam and Aaron are mentioned together on other occasions, his name comes first. Some scholars say this indicates Miriam was the instigator; she took the initiative in criticizing and questioning Moses, so she was the one that was punished.

Or perhaps God didn't want the tabernacle experience to be disrupted by the absence of Aaron, who was the high priest. If he had to move outside the camp, he would not have been available for ministry.

Even though he wasn't physically affected by God's judgment, he was affected as evident by what he said to Moses: "Please, sir, do not make *us* suffer this punishment for *our* foolish sin" (Numbers 12:11, author's emphasis). Aaron is convicted that he and Miriam did wrong. While he once saw their gripe about Moses as reasonable and legitimate, he now referred to it as "our foolish sin."

Aaron was terribly distraught over his sister's condition. He hated to see Miriam suffer. He could just imagine how terrible it was going to be: "like a still born infant coming from its mother's womb with its flesh half eaten away'" (Numbers 12:12 NIV). He was well aware of how awful leprosy can decompose the body, and he didn't want that for his sister.

Moses, too, cared about Miriam. "O God," he prayed, "heal her," and God did, although not immediately. For healing to be complete, she had to be isolated from the Israelite camp for seven days. After all, God said, "If her father had spit in her face, would she not have been in disgrace for seven days?" (Numbers 12:14 NIV).

Perhaps a period of isolation gave her time to think, to repent, and to have a heart change. While we don't know for certain this happened, we do know she learned from this experience. She learned her brothers appreciated her. They were both genuinely concerned about her, and she learned she had the respect of the whole nation.

The Israelites remained in place when Miriam was struck with a disease they all feared. They didn't say, *Miriam has leprosy. Let's get out of here!* They didn't break camp until Miriam was back in their midst as if to say *Miriam, we're here for you. We won't leave you behind. We value you.* Through this experience, Miriam learned she was appreciated, something she hadn't been able to feel when envy disturbed her heart.

What can we do if we find ourselves in a spot when we are tempted to be jealous or envious because someone else is receiving the glory? Or when we're not being appreciated? What can we do to change our heart? Here are some things we can do.

Get to know the person you envy. While Moses received credit and acclaim, he also had to deal with numerous gripes and complaints. While he played a grand role in the development of God's kingdom, his role was difficult. At one point, he was so exasperated he wanted God to kill him (see Numbers 11:15). Did they really want his life? Would they have really wanted to trade places with him? When we envy others, what we are often envying is an ideal version of them and their situation.

All you may know about the person you envy is their life from the outside. You don't know about the frustrations. You don't know about their pain. You don't know about the precipice of disasters they're standing on. Chances are you're envying someone whose life you wouldn't want if you got it—something you may discover when you get to know them better.

Give to others what you want to receive, or as Jesus put it, "Do for others what you want them to do for you" (Matthew 7:12). When you are wanting or needing praise, you probably are seeking a feeling of wholeness or confidence. Perhaps it's a sense of well-being you seek, so you can move forward with more confidence and feel that you are a person of worth. Interestingly, praising others can give you the same effect. Being a person who praises others, speaks words of encouragement, and does acts of kindness not only bolsters the recipient but bolsters you, the speaker, as well. Being kind with words or deeds—something to help someone else—can help you, too, if you are sincere and not manipulative.[1] The gladness which comes to your heart when someone praises you also comes when we show genuine interest in others.

Consider where you are in life. When you are feeling unappreciated, and envy sets in, it may be connected with where you are in life. I suggest this possibility because Miriam and Aaron were not young adults or petulant teenagers when they noticed their brother receiving more glory than they were. Miriam was the oldest of the three. If she was about twelve years old (some sources say seven) when Moses was born, and he spent forty years in Egypt, then another forty in the land of Midian before the escape from Egypt and the crossing of the Red Sea, then the three of them were old by the time envy struck. I feel like I can suggest this connection because "pathological jealousy is very common in both men and women over sixty years of age."[2]

As older people review their lives, looking back over the years, they may want to know (or be reassured) that their time here on earth mattered, that their life counted. As they think about this, they may compare themselves to others or envy those who are younger. They may measure the value of their life by the compliments or praises they receive. They may seek verification of their value through the words of others.

Of course, being an older adult isn't the only time in the life cycle when people feel a need for praise and recognition. You may need reassurance as you graduate from college or high school, when you turn thirty or any of the decade birthdays, or when the nest empties or fills up again! As we leave one stage and move on to the next, we may be frightened and unsure of ourselves. As one of my younger friends said, "I go kicking and screaming into the next stage." At those times, when life is changing, we could use some confidence building. Perhaps it's a signal we need to confess our fear and ask God for courage to embrace life's next stage instead of depending on the praise of others.

Perhaps we'll have to do as Miriam and Aaron had to learn to do—accept ourselves as having different callings and different ways of communicating. The apostle Paul determined, "We will not compare ourselves with each other as if one of us were better and another worse. We have far more interesting things to do with our lives."[3]

I'm inclined to think Miriam and Aaron learned from their experience because hundreds of years later, they were remembered by the prophet Micah as leaders of the nation of Israel along with Moses (see Micah 6:4). No distinction is made by Micah as to who was the most important. God called them all, and they were all valuable to God's deliverance of and formation of his people. Each was valuable in a different way—a thought to keep in mind when we start to think no one appreciates us or what we do. Who knows? Each of us is likely doing something that counts for all eternity.

Questions for Growth (Numbers 12:1–15 and Micah 6:4):

1. Have you started being critical when you are not usually a critical person? A fault finder? Why or how might this really be a jealousy, envy, or coveting issue?
2. Could age have something to do with Miriam and Aaron's criticism of Moses?
3. Were Miriam and Aaron wrong to think about credit? To think about their contributions?
4. What thoughts do you think Miriam had during her seven days of being "outside the camp"? What actions might she have taken?
5. Did Miriam and Aaron get answers to the questions: Why him? Why not us?
6. What does it say about Moses that he enjoyed God's favor (was a remarkable leader) yet remained humble?
7. How will this story help you to be more like Moses and less like Miriam and Aaron?
8. God defended Moses by citing his humility. How do you think God might defend you to those who are jealous or envious of you and express it through criticism? What would he have to say about you?
9. Is Miriam's and Aaron's experience teaching us we should never be critical? Is there ever a place for criticism?
10. What are some other examples of sibling conflict you see in Scripture?
11. Do you think Moses's not answering the criticism of Miriam and Aaron was a good way to handle it? Should Moses have defended himself?
12. God communicated with Miriam and Aaron through visions and dreams. How does God speak to you?

CHAPTER 6—ACHAN: OVERWHELMED BY WANTING

"Every time I go to church, I covet," I jokingly said to friends when Bob and I attended a storefront mission located across the street from a large furniture store with many display windows. Wherever we parked on Sunday, it was in front of a window. When getting out of the car, I couldn't help but look at the beautiful furniture on display. Sometimes an item would catch my eye, and I would move closer. As I did, an experience from my past surfaced. It came with a warning, "Be careful, Brenda, you know what could happen."

What Once Happened

When I was in seminary, one of my friends, Judy, and I would leave school and go to her aunt's house for a break. Judy, her aunt Susan,[1] and I would sit around the kitchen table, laughing, talking, and eating. As we did, my eyes were drawn to a large picture hanging on the wall above the table. The picture was of a large rooster made of various kinds of beans. Collages like this were popular at the time, but none of them interested me. This one, however, was very well done, and as I admired it, I wanted it.

Bob and I were engaged at the time, and so, I often thought ahead to the home we would have someday. As I gazed at the picture, I thought, *That's exactly the kind of picture I want in my kitchen*. Now I never said this out loud. I often, though, said things like this: "That picture is so nice," "I love that picture," or "What an attractive rooster!" Whether it was my intense gaze or those comments, it was clear to Aunt Susan I wanted the picture. She gave it to us as a wedding present.

Many months went by before Bob and I had a house with a kitchen where we were free to hang pictures. Before that, wherever we lived, we had the burden of storing the picture and seeing that it wasn't damaged. Finally, when we bought a house, we had a "just right" spot for hanging the bean collage. Up it went.

By this time, I was pregnant, and a friend loaned me some maternity clothes. The garments were of excellent quality, far beyond anything I could afford. It was a delight to wear them so imagine my disappointment one morning when I pulled a top out of the closet and saw small holes in it. I assumed I had snagged it on something and hadn't noticed.

The next day, however, the same thing happened with another top. I wondered, could something be wrong with our washing machine? In the days that followed, more damaged items appeared. It looked like something might be eating the clothes, so we called an exterminator. From him, we learned our house was infested with some kind of weevil.

To the exterminator, I stammered, "How?! How could this happen?"

He looked around the house and concluded it was through the bean picture. The varmints had moved in with us along with the picture. He said, "You're going to have to destroy the clothes in your closet and destroy the picture."

I hated seeing the clothes and the picture go up in flames. As I watched them burn, I stored the scene in my memory. From then on, it surfaced when I was tempted to covet, such as when standing in front of a furniture store window.

Coveting is a powerful emotion, and it has to be resisted, or it will overpower your will. It will take up residence in your heart, grow, dominate your thinking, rob you of peace and contentment, and possibly lead to wrong actions as it did in Achan's case. When he saw items he wanted, he didn't resist, and it caused trouble for him, his family, and his fellow Israelites.

Who Was Achan?

Achan was an Israelite soldier—one of many soldiers under the leadership of Joshua as God's people entered the Promised Land. While the land was promised to the Israelites, they had to fight for it. That the land was promised meant God would help them be victorious. With that assurance, they proceeded with confidence. They were certain they could take the land, and they did at first when they captured Jericho.

When the fighting was over and victory secured, Joshua admonished his solders to refrain from looting. They were not to take any spoils of war. Joshua said to them, "The city and everything in it must be totally destroyed as an offering to the Lord ... you are not to take anything that is to be destroyed; if you do, you will bring trouble and destruction on the Israelite camp. Everything made of silver, gold, bronze, or iron is set apart for the Lord. It is to be put in the Lord's treasury" (Joshua 6:17–19). While this may seem drastic to us, the purpose was to purge the land of idol worship and other pagan practices which might tempt God's people when they occupied the land.

As Achan looked around at all the debris from fighting, some things caught his eyes:

- A beautiful Babylonian garment, probably a cloak or a robe of some kind.
- Two hundred shekels of silver (about 5 pounds of silver).
- A bar of gold that weighed over one pound.

When Achan *saw* these things, he "*coveted* them, and *took* them" (Joshua 7:21, KJV, author's emphasis). He ignored the tenth commandment which says, "You shall not covet *your neighbor's house*. You shall not covet *your neighbor's wife*, or his male or female *servant*, his *ox* or donkey, or any*thing* that belongs to your neighbor" (Exodus 20:17 NIV, author's emphasis). If coveting isn't controlled, it can lead to wrong action, as Achan's experience illustrates.

Why would Achan take these things when he knew he wasn't supposed to? There appeared to be no extenuating circumstances such as poverty or necessity that might shed light on his motive. He may have thought about how delicious his life was going to be once the items were in his possession. How nice he would look in the cloak. Friends would ooh and aah. How envious they would be when he tossed around some of the silver shekels or held up the gold bar for everyone to see. But obviously he couldn't do those things because he had to hide the items so he wouldn't be caught.

As far as Achan knew, no Israelite saw him take the items, but God saw, and his anger burned against Achan *and* all the Israelites. As a result, they lost their protective covering. When they moved on to Ai, the next place they planned to conquer, they expected an easy victory because Ai was smaller than Jericho. They didn't even send the whole army because they were so confident the outcome would be in their favor. The attack, though, ended in disaster. The Israelites were routed and thirty-six soldiers died.

Joshua and his men were shocked. They were God's people. How could this happen? They were so grieved they tore their clothes and threw themselves to the ground in front of the Ark of the Covenant—the box that contained the Ten Commandments including the commandment "Thou shall not covet." The men lay there till evening with dust on their heads showing their disappointment.

Joshua himself was in deep distress. He cried out to God. He questioned why he brought them to the Promised Land in the first place if he was going to treat them this way. He worried about what was going to happen now that Ai had beaten them. What did this defeat mean for their future? He said, "The Canaanites and everyone else in the country will hear about it. They will surround us and kill every one of us!" (Joshua 7:9).

God informed Joshua the ban on taking any possessions from Jericho had been violated. He said he would withhold support from the Israelite army until the stolen property was recovered. God told Joshua to gather the Israelites, conduct an investigation, and find the guilty party. When they did, the Israelites discovered it was Achan. He had stolen the cloak, the silver coins, and the gold bar.

Joshua said to Achan, "Why have you brought such trouble on us? The Lord will now bring trouble on you!" (Joshua 7:25).

The Israelites "stoned Achan to death; they also stoned and burned his family and possessions" (Joshua 7:25). When this was completed, God was no longer angry with the people, and Joshua and the Israelite troops went on to be victorious at Ai.

While Achan's story helps us understand the power of coveting and the need for punishment to correct a sinful situation, you may be left wondering as I am about why Achan's family had to be punished. He was the one who was guilty, so why was the family punished too?

One possibility is they may have been aware of Achan's crime. It's doubtful he would have had his own personal tent—more likely he hid the loot in the family tent. This would have been difficult to do without being observed.

A second possibility is the family may have been punished along with Achan because at the time, a person was considered important and significant only in relation to a group. One person's blessing resulted in blessings on the group. One person's guilt revealed the guilt of the entire family.

Those are two possible explanations. There may be others. I don't know the exact reason, but I know this—there's a spiritual truth here. In one sense, our sins, including coveting, are strictly between us and God (see Psalm 51:4). In another sense, though, our wanting—if not controlled—can affect the lives of others, particularly those we interact with, live with, partner with, work with, or worship with.

For example, a person steals something because, like Achan, he covets it. Even if he isn't caught, his having to keep it a secret requires emotional energy and concentration to keep what he's done hidden. He can't fully give himself to others because he must keep covered what he has done. If he is caught, he will bring disgrace on his wife, his children, and even his parents. If he is punished and goes to jail, he takes his earning power with him, and family members have to pick up the slack. While he is away, his children are robbed of his presence and his guidance.

That coveting can have visible, disturbing consequences is something Ginny, in her thirties and single, needed to realize. When I met her at a conference, she didn't say much while several of us talked informally after a session about jealousy, envy, and coveting. Later Ginny caught up with me in the hallway and said, "Can we talk?"

"Sure," I responded. "What's on your mind?"

She said, "When we were talking, I realized I might be guilty of coveting."

"Oh, how's that?"

"I find myself dropping by my friend's house so I can be around her husband. Ken's so funny, so warm, and so engaging in his personality. Heather's usually busy with the children, so he and I end up at the kitchen table drinking coffee together. At those times, I can't help but wish Ken were my husband."

Not knowing quite how to respond, I said, "Ginny, do you have any idea why you feel the way you do?"

Ginny didn't respond immediately, but I could see her mental wheels turning. I waited. After a while, she said, "I guess what I really want is a husband. All the girls in my high school group are married but me. One by one, as they married, I always assumed I would someday, although I've never dated much. I often imagine what it would be like to have a mate, someone I could easily talk with and who would make me feel warm and loved. Ken makes me feel that way, and when I'm around him, I painfully realize what I'm missing ..."

Her voice trailed off, and she looked off into the distance. When she looked back, she said, "I'm thirty-seven, and I feel like time is running out for finding a mate."

In her early twenties, coveting her friend's husband was never a problem for Ginny. There was still time. Now nearing forty, she felt her chances for getting married diminishing. With this insight, we were able to talk about what would happen if she continued to want her friend's husband. She might experience perpetual discontent, never having a heart at peace. She would cut herself off from finding someone to marry. Or, unchecked, she could even be tempted to try to break up her friend's marriage.

I don't know if talking about those consequences was enough to motivate her to cease coveting, because I never saw Ginny again after that conference. I do know recalling the consequences of my bean picture experience helped me on Sunday mornings. While I wasn't pausing long, I was stopping long enough that *wanting* started interfering with my worship. That's why I quit looking in the windows on the way to church, and that's why to me, coveting is no joking matter.

Questions for Growth (Joshua 7:1–26):

1. Why did God tell Joshua to quit praying? (7:10–13)
2. How long do you think Achan thought about the cloak, the silver and the gold before he took them?
3. Why did the Israelites need to purge the camp (7:1)?
4. What did Joshua seek from Achan? (7:19)?
5. What would have happened if Achan's sin hadn't been dealt with?
6. What kinds of consequences occur in our lives when we sin and try to hide it?
7. What corporate bodies or groups do you belong to that may be affected by your *wanting*?
8. Since Achan couldn't really do anything with what he coveted and took, what joy or pleasure did he get from taking what was forbidden?
9. Do you think telling someone not to take something makes them want it even more?
10. What are some examples of how the behavior of one person can have significant repercussions on a larger group?
11. Why do you think Achan sinned, even though he knew God's orders? Isn't knowing what is wrong enough to keep us from acting on our wanting impulses?
12. Apparently, Achan didn't stop to consider why he wanted the items "so much that [he] took them" (7:21). What are some questions he should have asked himself—questions that might have stopped him from taking what wasn't his?

CHAPTER 7—SAUL: WHEN JEALOUSY RAGES

What we *see* that makes us jealous, envious, or covetous doesn't have to be an object, an action, or a scene right in front of us. What we *see* can be something that occurs in the mind's eye—something visible only to us. This inner picture can be triggered by any number of things. For Saul, it was what he *heard*.

The Sound of Comparison

Saul was the first king of the nation of Israel. He didn't seek this role; he was chosen. He was out looking for lost donkeys when Samuel, a prophet and priest, spotted him. At God's direction, Samuel anointed Saul to be king. Samuel even stayed in the area and guided Saul in his new role.

The people responded well to Saul. He was tall, handsome, and daring, so the people readily followed him. They sensed he had all the qualities necessary to be their leader.

With the blessing of God, the guidance of Samuel, and the favorable response of the people, Saul could have thrived in the role and been a successful king. He might have if he hadn't *heard* some women singing.

At the time, Saul was dealing with his biggest challenge as Israel's leader—the Philistines. This fierce, cruel people continually harassed God's people. Fear prevailed. One person, though, who wasn't terrified by the Philistines was a young Israelite named David.

Saul became acquainted with David when he entered the royal palace as a harpist to play for him. He really got Saul's attention, though, when he killed the Philistine giant, Goliath. Noticing David's fearlessness, Saul made him an officer in his army and sent him on missions.

One day when Saul, David, and the soldiers were returning home from successfully fighting the Philistines, women from every town in Israel came out to meet them.

They sang joyful songs, danced, and played tambourines and lyres. As they danced, the women sang. This is what they sang: "Saul has slain his thousands, and David his tens of thousands" (1 Samuel 18:7 NIV). This is what Saul heard: *David better than I? More successful than I, their king*?!

Saul was infuriated. He didn't like being compared with David and coming up short. As king, he should receive the highest praise. The best accolades should be for him. Rather than shrugging his shoulders and moving forward, he dwelt on what he heard. A picture formed in his mind. Saul *saw* the people making David king, and he was certain this is what the outcome would be. Upon hearing this song one time on one occasion, he concluded the people wanted David to be king. From there he assumed this was all David's fault, that he was already siphoning things off to himself. Saul asked himself, "What more can he get but the kingdom?" (1 Samuel 18:8 NIV). He was convinced David was interfering with what was rightly his and was going to take even more. Saul was determined to protect what was his. "So he was jealous and suspicious of David from that day on" (1 Samuel 18:9).

As he did, Saul's jealousy grew and attracted other emotions:

Suspicion. Saul watched David's every move, because any day he might try to take over the throne.

Fear. If David could take down a giant, what else was he capable of doing?

Worry. If David could get this kind of acclaim now, what more can he get?

Resentment. David was interfering with Saul's role, taking accolades that should be his.

Left unchecked, emotions like these can turn into a volatile mix. They did for Saul. The next day after hearing the women sing, Saul "raved in his house like a madman (1 Samuel 18:10). David attempted to soothe him by playing the harp. But Saul, who was fiddling with a spear, suddenly hurled it at David. Saul said to himself, "I'll pin him to the wall" (18:11). He threw the spear not once but twice. Fortunately, David dodged each time and escaped.

Next, Saul tried sending David away and put him in command of a thousand men. Perhaps he thought, *That will take care of him for a while*. But it didn't. It only increased Saul's fear because David was successful in all the battles he and his men fought. Saul noticed and "became even more afraid of him" (1 Samuel 18:15). Saul tried in numerous ways to get rid of David, even actually pursuing him, but he was unsuccessful.

Saul's jealousy kept him from seeing that David was a great asset. David was a skillful harpist whose music soothed Saul, a great warrior in Saul's army, and a loyal subject. Saul should have numbered David among his greatest blessings. Instead Saul regarded him as his greatest obstacle, standing in the way of his being a king extolled by the people.

If it weren't for David, I would have the admiration of the people

If it weren't for David, I would be a successful king.

If it weren't for David, I would be Israel's hero.

If it weren't for David, I wouldn't have to worry about losing the throne.

Saul's preoccupation with David interfered with his being a capable leader at a time when Israel needed to be strong. It eventually prompted Saul to embark on an ill-conceived battle which he lost. His despair was so great, his disappointment so keen, that he took his own life. What a shame.

If only he hadn't seen David as his enemy, how differently things might have turned out.

If only he hadn't nursed and replayed what he heard the women sing over and over.

If only he hadn't let his jealousy grow and take on other emotions. How different his story might have been!

Saul was a strong man with leadership potential that was recognized by God, Samuel, and the people. What could possibly explain how he could be so vulnerable to what he heard?

Scripture suggests three possible explanations:

Saul's self-image. When Samuel spotted Saul and a servant looking for some lost donkeys, he indicated to Saul their meeting was very significant. That should have perked up Saul's ears and make his heart beat with confidence, but Saul resisted Samuel's opinion. He said, "I belong to the tribe of Benjamin, the smallest tribe in Israel, and my family is the least important one in the tribe. Why, then, do you talk like this to me?" (1 Samuel 9:21).

When Samuel called all the Israelites together to announce Saul's kingship appointment publicly, Saul could not be found. Eventually they discovered him "*hiding* behind the supplies" (1 Samuel 10:22, author's italics). He just didn't see himself in this important role.

While Samuel and the people saw Saul with leadership qualities, Saul didn't see himself in the same way. The words of the singing women confirmed what inwardly he had known all along about himself—he wasn't up to handling a leadership role. Therefore, he couldn't or wouldn't slough off what he heard, as a person with a healthier self-image might be able to do.

Saul's disobedience. While Saul was being guided by God through Samuel, Saul didn't always follow Samuel's directions. After Saul was king, Samuel told him to go to Gilgal and wait for him there. He would come later and offer sacrifices. At that time, Samuel would tell Saul what God wanted him to do next. Saul didn't wait.

On another occasion, Samuel told Saul to destroy the Amalekites, another enemy of the Israelites. Samuel instructed Saul to kill every one of them, even their sheep, cattle and camels. Saul destroyed the Amalekites, but he didn't kill their commander, and he kept alive the best of their cattle.

Because of Saul's refusals to follow Samuel's guidance—in essence, this was the same as disobeying God—God chose David as king. When Samuel gave Saul the news, he said, "You rejected the Lord's command, and he has rejected you as king of Israel" (1 Samuel 15:26b). He told him David would be the next king. The words of the singing women might have stirred up his jealousy because he was painfully aware that he was no longer God's choice.

Saul's distress. When Samuel turned his attention to David, anointing him as Israel's next king, God's Spirit left Saul, and "an evil spirit sent by the Lord tormented him" (1 Samuel 16:14). That God would send an evil spirit sounds rather shocking to us. We must remember, though, that at this time in the history of God's people, everything—good and evil—was attributed to the Lord. In time they—and we—have come to understand that an adversary, Satan, affects people adversely.

What this evil spirit might mean is Saul became depressed when God chose David to be Israel's king.[1] I say this because of the black moods he experienced. If you have ever been depressed (as I have been), you understand how wretched you can feel. In this state, it is easy to blame others. *If it weren't for him—or her—I wouldn't be so miserable.* It's easy to lose perspective (*I'm no longer valuable*) or over-generalize (*there's no place for me now*).

Saul's black moods weren't something only he was aware of; his servants were too. When they witnessed darkness descending, they offered to "look for a man who knows how to play the harp. Then when the evil spirit comes on you, the man can play his harp, and you will be all right again" (1 Samuel 16:16). That's when they found David, an accomplished harpist, and brought him into the palace to play for Saul. As he listened to the music, "the evil spirit would leave, and Saul would feel better and be all right again" (16:23).

Saul could have had bipolar depression. This would explain the times of mania (*I'll pin him to the wall!*) and the times of lowness (the black moods). Anyone struggling with a mental illness such as bipolar disease or major depression is vulnerable to what others say—they don't always process their thoughts accurately. That's the nature of these conditions, but mentally healthy people shouldn't consider themselves impervious to being affected by what others say. Any of us at any time can entertain in our head images prompted by something we hear and what we see. As Peter Toohey writes in his book, *Jealousy*, "Ears mishear and eyes magnify."[2] They can both prompt us to be miserable about our situations or how we view ourselves.

I don't know if any one of these three suggested explanations—or even a combination of the three—is why Saul kept a jealous eye on David. What I do know is that considering the explanations started me questioning why I was experiencing pangs of jealousy.

Was it due to low self-esteem? I didn't think so, but who couldn't improve in how they view themselves? Surely the pangs didn't have anything to do with my relationship with God. I was a born-again, spirit-filled Christian, a daily Bible reader, a strong pray-er, and an active church member. I was being as obedient to God's will as I knew how to be. Or was it depression? As I mentioned, I had experienced depression, had researched and even written a book about it. I was so familiar with the symptoms I could honestly say being depressed didn't explain my pangs of jealousy. I might become depressed, though, if I couldn't figure out what was behind the pangs. They were increasing in frequency, so I was determined to press on in studying what the Bible had to say about jealousy, envy, and coveting. Somewhere in there was an answer for me, and I believe answers for all of us when our hearts are disturbed by what we see and what we hear.

Questions for Growth (1 Samuel 18:6–16):

1. When have you said or thought, "If it weren't for ____"? Was this in relation to your job, your marriage, or your friendships? What's dangerous about using the words "If it weren't for ____" in your thoughts or in your verbal conversations?
2. Some people readily shrug off what they hear others say, then go on and forget about what was heard. Others don't. What makes the difference?
3. Why do you think some people keep what they hear alive and let their comments influence their outlook on life and their hope for the future?
4. Would Saul's reaction to the women's praises be so extreme if he had not been an insecure person?
5. What would have been a better way for Saul to respond to the singers' comparison of him and David than being jealous?
6. What did Saul miss by not appreciating David?
7. How can Saul's story encourage us to not compare ourselves to others?
8. At what point in the progression of Saul's jealousy should he have tried to stop his thoughts from escalating? What are ways we can keep from letting our thoughts grow and become harmful to ourselves or to others?
9. Why does jealousy or envy sometimes bring out a cruel streak in a person?
10. If Saul had fully accepted who he was, what difference would it have made in his relationship with David? In his being king? In his relationship with God?
11. If Saul could have seen himself the way God saw him, what difference might it have made in his life? In his happiness? In his being a successful leader?

CHAPTER 8—DAVID: WRONG DESIRES, WRONG ACTIONS

Remember how we applauded the virtues of David in the last chapter? He soothed the dark moods of King Saul with his harp playing, he killed the Philistine giant, Goliath, he was victorious in numerous battles, and he was always loyal to the king. David was smart, strong, and brave. He was well liked by the people and attracted numerous followers.

In addition, David was a spiritually sensitive man, "a man after his [God's] own heart" (1 Samuel 13:14 KJV), and he looked after the interests of God's people. He completed the occupation of the Promised Land and extended its boundaries. He established Jerusalem as Israel's capital city and brought the Tabernacle there so God's people could have a central place of worship.

It's hard to believe that someone like this—so spiritual, so strong, so well liked, and so effective as a leader—could *want* something or someone so badly he would break God's commandments, but he did.

What was David thinking?!

I don't think he intentionally meant to break God's laws. I don't believe he had sinning in mind when he got up from a nap one spring day and went up to the roof of his palace. Usually he would have been away fighting with the Israelite troops, but this time he had stayed behind. As he walked around on the rooftop, David had a wide view. From this high position, he saw "a woman taking a bath in her house" (2 Samuel 11:2). He should have turned his gaze away and looked elsewhere or left the roof altogether, but he didn't. David was mesmerized by her beauty. *Who is this woman*? He had to know. David sent a messenger to find out.

When the messenger returned, he said the woman's name was Bathsheba, and she was married to Uriah the Hittite, an officer who was away fighting as a part of David's army. That she was married should have ended David's interest. He knew the tenth commandment: "Thou shall not covet thy neighbor's wife" (Exodus 20:17 KJV). Apparently, though, the commandment didn't enter his mind. He was consumed with desire—a desire that led to several wrong actions.

Wrong action #1—David committed adultery.

When he was told she was married, he should not have made any effort to contact her, let alone have her brought to the palace. Instead, he sent messengers to fetch Bathsheba. They "brought her to him" (2 Samuel 11:4) and David "slept with her" (2 Samuel 11:4 NIV). Afterward, Bathsheba went back home.

It wasn't long before Bathsheba sent a message to David saying she was pregnant. The Bible says she "had just finished her monthly ritual of purification" (2 Samuel 11:4) before sleeping with David. This information is to let readers know the baby was indeed David's. No doubt about it. Her message to David led to David's next wrong action.

Wrong action #2—David attempted to cover up his sin.

There were people who knew she had visited the palace. David was going to be found out. He attempted to cover up the fact he was responsible for Bathsheba's pregnancy by arranging for her husband to return home. He assumed Uriah would sleep with his wife while home. That way, when the child was born, Uriah—and everyone else—would think the child was his.

When Uriah arrived, David engaged him in conversation, and then he told him to go home and rest.

Uriah, though, didn't return home. He spent the night at the entrance of the royal palace, in the company of other army officers.

The next morning, David summoned Uriah and questioned him about why he didn't go home for the night.

Uriah answered, "The men of Israel and Judah are away in battle ... my commander Joab and his officers are camping out in the open. How could I go home, eat and drink, and sleep with my wife? By all that's sacred, I swear that I could never do such a thing!" (2 Samuel 11:11).

Beads of perspiration surely popped up on David's forehead as he realized his plan might fail. Panicking, David instructed Uriah to remain in Jerusalem for a second day, and David spent the day with him eating and drinking. By evening, Uriah was drunk. David thought, *surely now he will go home to Bathsheba*. But he didn't. He just couldn't do it because the other officers didn't have the same opportunity.

When David's efforts at covering up his sin didn't work, he tried something else, which resulted in yet another wrong action.

Wrong Action #3—David caused innocent people to be killed.

When David sent Uriah back to the battlefront, he sent a letter along with him for Joab, his commander. It said, "Put Uriah in the front line, where the fighting is heaviest, then retreat and let him be killed'" (2 Samuel 11:15).

Joab, a loyal David follower, acted promptly. He put Uriah, along with some of the other troops, in a position where they had to confront enemy soldiers. The two sides fought. Just as David wanted, Uriah was killed along with several other officers.

Joab immediately sent a messenger with a full report of the battle to David. He specifically instructed the messenger to tell the king that Uriah was among those killed.

Once back in Jerusalem, the messenger described the battle and informed David that several officers including Uriah were killed. David didn't grieve or even appear concerned. He sent the messenger back to Joab with a callous message: "You never can tell who will die in battle" (2 Samuel 11:25). It's hard to believe those heartless words could come out of the mouth of someone who was spiritually sensitive and had pleased God so much of his life.

God "was not pleased with what David had done" this time (2 Samuel 11:27). Yet David seemed unaware of God's displeasure. While we don't know for sure (the Old Testament doesn't always reveal the feelings of its characters as it tells their stories), David didn't appear to harbor any guilt or remorse for what he had done. It's almost as if David was impervious to the idea that he had done anything wrong. His conscience needed to be pricked and God had just the person to do that.

God's Spokesperson

God sent his prophet Nathan to help David see he was guilty. He didn't, though, say, "David, you are guilty of coveting, adultery, and murder," which was wise. When a person denies acknowledging sin as David appeared to be doing, you can't just say to him or her, "You are guilty," and expect them to repent. The person would probably go on the defensive: "No, I didn't do it." Something is needed to arouse their emotions, prick their conscience, and alert them to their wrongdoing. Nathan did this with a story.

Nathan sought out David on the pretext of seeking his advice about a troubling situation. He said, "There were two men who lived in the same town; one was rich and the other poor. The rich man had many cattle and sheep, while the poor man had only one lamb, which he had bought. He took care of it, and it grew up in his home with his children.

He would feed it some of his own food, let it drink from his cup, and hold it in his lap. The lamb was like a daughter to him. One day a visitor arrived at the rich man's home. The rich man didn't want to kill one of his own animals to fix a meal for him; instead, he took the poor man's lamb and prepared a meal for his guest" (2 Samuel 12:1–4).

Upon hearing this story, David flew into a rage. He said, "I swear by the living Lord that the man who did this ought to die! For having done such a cruel thing, he must pay back four times as much as he took" (2 Samuel 12:5–6).

David could see the injustice in this situation and determined the rich man deserved punishment. Nathan was now in a position to point the finger of guilt, which he did. "'You are that man,' Nathan said to David" (2 Samuel 12:7). Now that he had David's attention, he spelled out what God had done for him and what would happen as a result of his wrong actions.

Nathan reminded David that God had blessed him in numerous ways.

- God rescued him numerous times from Saul.
- God gave David his kingdom.
- God gave him wives.
- God made him king over Israel and Judah.

Then Nathan told him that he was going to regret his wrong actions. He would suffer as a result of his sins.

- "In every generation some of your descendants will die a violent death" (2 Samuel 12:10).
- "Someone from your own family" will "bring trouble on you" (2 Samuel 12:11).
- God will take "your wives from you and give them to another man" (2 Samuel 12:11).
- The other man "will have intercourse with them in broad daylight" (2 Samuel 12:11).

Finally, shamed and weakened by Nathan's strong words, David admitted he was guilty. He said, "I have sinned against the Lord" (2 Samuel 12:13). He understood he could not wipe away his coveting, his adultery, and his having Uriah and others killed.

Does this mean God didn't forgive David? No, Nathan reassured David that he was forgiven—he wasn't going to die for his sins, but it did mean his wrong actions would have consequences. Just as Nathan predicted, his actions cost him years of unhappiness and grief. In addition to what Nathan predicted, the child he and Bathsheba conceived died because David had "shown such contempt for the Lord" (2 Samuel 12:14).

David's experience reminds us even the best of us, even those of us who have been Christ followers for a long time, and even those of us who are richly blessed, can have wrong desires. While how we live and follow God provides great insulation against having wrong desires, we can never assume we won't be tempted. If we are, what are some things we can learn from David's story to help us keep wrong desires from turning into wrong actions?

Stop looking at the object of your attraction. When David saw a woman bathing, he should have turned his head. When we covet someone, we need to avoid fixing our attention on the person either in face-to-face encounters or in our mind. Once an attraction begins, we can *see* the person in our mind and start fantasizing about interacting. You feel free to do this because you think you are not really hurting anyone, or you are not sinning because no action is ever taken, but it is sin, and it needs to be dealt with and stopped.

Consider the consequences. When David learned Bathsheba was married, he should have stopped and thought about what might happen if he acted on his desire. He was an intelligent man; he should have realized defying God's commandments could complicate his life. A friend of mine learned this the hard way. Angela was attracted to another man and had a brief affair—one her husband happened to learn about. Ever since, each time she and her husband have any kind of conflict—the kind two people sometimes have in living and working together—he throws her past adultery in her face. He does this angrily and with such force she's left feeling weak for days afterwards. He refuses to forget what happened even though she's been a faithful wife ever since. How much better her marriage would be today if she had turned away from her wrong desire, instead of letting it lead to wrong action.

Talk to God. When Nathan, as God's spokesman, outlined to David the ways in which God had blessed him, he said, "And if all this had been too little, I would have given you even more" (2 Samuel 12:8 NIV). Through Nathan, I believe God was saying to David, "If something was missing from your life, if some need wasn't being met, if you had come to me, I would have supplied your need." I doubt David had a sexual need since he already had wives. Perhaps there was something else going on in his life that prompted him to act so recklessly. After all, he was in Jerusalem when he should have been with his troops. Did this indicate he was going through some form of malaise? Was life losing its excitement? The adrenalin no longer flowing as it once did? If so, perhaps this is one time when David should have expressed his feelings to God as his psalms indicate he did on so many other occasions.

Just as something else might have been going on in David's life, there might be something else going on in our lives to cause us to be influenced by the power of wanting. Whether there is or isn't, Nathan's words to David encourage us to reveal our hearts to God. Expressing to him what is happening in our lives doesn't necessarily mean we will get an immediate understanding of why we desire what we do and the need behind it. We may or we may not. The answer may take a while, because some heart issues need time to be resolved. What it does mean—and why talking with God is so important—is that we open ourselves for God to do a work of grace in our lives. We give him the opportunity to strengthen us so our wrong desires will not result in wrong actions that will complicate our life.

Questions for Growth (2 Samuel 11:1-12:15):

1. How many of the Ten Commandments did David break? Which ones were they?
2. David's seeing Bathsheba was probably unintentional, but at what point could he or should he have stopped the escalation that led to adultery, manipulation and murder?
3. When has the Lord been displeased with something you have wanted?
4. Why is confronting our guilt important? Why is admitting wrong important to getting past moments of infidelity and preventing future episodes?
5. Why is sexual temptation hard to resist? How does culture contribute to being tempted sexually?
6. What people were hurt as a result of David's coveting?
7. What do you think would have happened to David if he hadn't finally admitted to being a sinner?
8. Is covetousness, an old-fashioned word and one seldom used, still prevalent in society today? In what areas do you see it occurring? What might tempt a Christian to covet?
9. Nathan said David showed "contempt for the Lord" (12:14). What does that mean?
10. Why is talking with God so important in dealing with wrong desires?

CHAPTER 9—AHAB: WHEN YOUR FACE REVEALS YOUR HEART

When our oldest sons were nine and seven, we moved to the Promised Land. Well, at least my husband and I thought of it that way. The rural home we purchased held the promise of an ideal environment for boys.

We had been living in a suburb where houses were close together. Each house had a small front yard and a fenced backyard. Parked cars lined both sides of the streets. This left little room for Jim and Joel to play. If they played ball in the streets—which was dangerous—the balls hit cars and neighbors complained. If they played soccer in the backyard, the ball often landed in a neighbor's yard. Jim or Joel would have to go next door to get someone to retrieve the ball.

To provide our sons a freer environment, we moved to the country. The house we bought was situated on 1.6 acres, with a wooded area in back and a pond on one side. We co-owned the pond with neighbors living on the other side. Our side was bordered by a chain-link fence; theirs was not.

With so much open space, the boys could play ball and not be in danger of being hit by cars. They could play soccer without bothering the neighbors. They could fish in the pond and maybe get a rowboat someday. In the wooded area, the boys could use their imagination to play jungle or cowboys. Bob and I were certain we had found an ideal environment for boys, but they didn't see it that way.

What they saw was the neighbors having fun—fun they weren't part of. The neighbors had a swimming pool, which in their eyes was much better than a pond. Their children had dirt bikes and mopeds. Our sons watched them ride around and around their property. Jim and Joel spent hours clinging to the chain-link fence, gazing longingly across the pond. No matter how much Bob and I reminded them of the fun possibilities in their own yard, they wanted what the neighbors had. Interestingly, they never said this out loud. They didn't have to; their faces said it all. Their *wanting* was as evident as Ahab's when he *wanted* what someone else had.

Who Was Ahab?

Ahab was an Israelite king who reigned in Samaria. He was the wealthy owner of several properties including houses and land. His winter palace was in Jezreel, which is where he was when he noticed a beautiful vineyard next to his property.

As he looked at the vineyard bordering his land, he began dreaming of how nice it would be to have this property. He thought it would make an ideal place for a vegetable garden. He saw it, he wanted it, and so he set out to get it.

How he went about it was reasonable. He went to see Naboth, the vineyard owner. Ahab told Naboth he wanted his land, what he planned to do with it, and made him an offer. He said, "Let me have your vineyard; it is close to my palace, and I want to use the land for a vegetable garden. I will give you a better vineyard for it or, if you prefer, I will pay you fair price'" (1 Kings 21:2).

Naboth wasn't interested in relocating or selling. From the time the Israelites conquered the Promised Land, Naboth's land had belonged to his family. He said to Ahab, "I inherited this vineyard from my ancestors" and "the Lord forbid that I should let you have it!" (1 Kings 21:3).

Naturally, Ahab was disappointed. Most people would have been. If you see something that would better your situation, and you make what you feel is a decent offer, but your offer is refused, you naturally feel let down. But you get over the disappointment and move on. That's the nature of life. Some people, though, don't react that way. When the desire is strong and then denied, they want the item even more. They don't let it go, which is what happened with Ahab.

The way Ahab saw it, Naboth was a mere commoner standing in the way of his getting what he wanted, when as king, it should be available to him. He felt powerless and deprived: *How could Naboth have refused me, the king? I made him a fair offer. He could build a vineyard at any number of other places. Why did he have to be so rigid? I want that land, and it should be mine.*

Brooding like this doesn't bring relief. Instead, the feeling of deprivation grows in strength and attracts other feelings. In addition to coveting, Ahab became "depressed and angry" (1 Kings 21:4) and it was evident. Ahab "lay down on his bed, facing the wall, and would not eat" (21:4).

Anyone walking by could see something was wrong with Ahab even if they were unaware of his dealings with Naboth. While some people can hide their feelings, others can't or won't. This is particularly true of jealousy and envy as cultural references show. The root meaning of the Hebrew word for jealousy is to become red in the face. Shakespeare called jealousy the green-eyed monster, but we also talk about people being green with envy. In his book, *Envy*, Joe Epstein wrote that "envy is cross-, squinty-, and blearily red-eyed."[1]

I had to chuckle at another comment Epstein made. He said, "Envy causes a choking feeling in the throat" that "squeezes the eyes out of their sockets."[2] When I read that, I remembered a woman in charge of a conference where I was speaking. When it came time for giving the door prize, she showed the audience what the prize was. Her eyes weren't quite out of their sockets, but they were close as she described the prize. Obviously, she would like to have it. As she talked, she held the basket containing the names of the participants. She shuffled the slips of paper, and then drew out the name of the winner. Usually a host lets an uninvolved participant do the drawing for the sake of fairness. But this woman did the selecting herself, and you guessed correctly, she pulled out her own name. She kept the prize. None of us were surprised because her eyes had already told us what was coming.

While Ahab's wanting may have started with envy or coveting, the denial of what he wanted led to other feelings. He became "depressed and angry over what Naboth ... said to him" (1 Kings 21:4). These feelings, too, can be revealed in your face or in your body language. Your face may be flushed with anger, or you may have a somber look or a furrowed brow. Your discontent may be reflected in your countenance like Cain's was. "His countenance fell" (Genesis 4:5b KJV), and "he scowled in anger" (Genesis 4:5).

Besides showing in your face, your feelings may also be evident in the way you hold yourself, the way your shoulders sag, or even the way you walk. In Ahab's case, he went to bed, turned his face toward the wall, and sulked. Everything about his body language indicated something was wrong. His wife, Queen Jezebel, noticed. She said, "What's wrong with you?"

"He answered, 'Because of what Naboth said to me. I offered to buy his vineyard or, if he preferred, to give him another one for it, but he told me that I couldn't have it!'" (1 Kings 21:6). Sounds like a spoiled child, doesn't he?

Jezebel was shocked by his answer. She wasn't an Israelite; she was the daughter of a tyrannical Phoenician king. Inconceivable to her was that a king's desire could be frustrated by one of his subjects. She railed at Ahab: "'Well, are you the king or aren't you? ... Get out of bed, cheer up, and eat'" (1 Kings 21:7).

Actually, her words contained good advice for someone depressed and sullen:

Get out of bed—fight the lethargy that goes with depression and sulking.

Cheer up—work on your attitude, all is not lost.

Eat—get some nourishment so you'll have more energy.

While her suggestions were spot-on, Jezebel was impatient. She didn't wait for Ahab to follow her advice. She said, "'I will get you Naboth's vineyard!'" (1 Kings 21:7). And she did, but in a totally unfair way.

Jezebel had the officials and leading citizens of Jezreel organize a gathering, invite Naboth and give him a place of honor. She also told them to get a couple of scoundrels to be present and to accuse Naboth of cursing God and the king. While she would not be present, she knew the gathering would declare Naboth guilty of blasphemy.

Her plan worked. Naboth was falsely accused, found guilty, and was immediately stoned to death. At that time, when people were convicted of blasphemy, they lost their estates as well as their lives, so when Jezebel got word that Naboth was dead, she rushed to Ahab with the news. She said to him, "Now go and take possession of the vineyard which he refused to sell you" (1 Kings 21:15). That news got Ahab up off the bed. Immediately, he went to claim Naboth's vineyard. Unbeknownst to Ahab, someone else was heading there at the same time.

Surprise!

God told Elijah, the prophet, to go to Naboth's vineyard. He said, "Ask Ahab, 'After murdering the man [Naboth], are you taking over his property as well?'" (1 Kings 21:19). Neither Ahab nor Jezebel actually threw the stones that killed Naboth, but in God's eyes, they were guilty of murder. Elijah told Ahab he and Jezebel would be punished. Their family would be affected—God would get rid of every male in his family, young and old alike. He said Ahab and Jezebel would die where Naboth died, and dogs would lick up their blood.

The punishment was so shocking to Ahab that "When Elijah finished speaking, Ahab tore his clothes, took them off, and put on sackcloth. He refused food, slept in the sackcloth, and went about gloomy and depressed" (1 Kings 21:27). This time, depression and gloom were appropriate. He had sinned, and his countenance indicated he was grieved and sorry. Therefore, God mercifully postponed punishment for a time, but eventually the events happened as Elijah predicted. Judgment could have been avoided if Ahab hadn't coveted, pouted, and let Jezebel take over and arrange Naboth's death. As king, Ahab had lots of power and therefore, many choices. There were other places he could have cultivated a vegetable garden. In that sense, he was like our sons who were so focused on what they didn't have, they couldn't appreciate what they did have. They were children, though, and didn't know better. They learned and came to enjoy the space, the pond, and the woods behind the house.

As adults, we don't want to be so enamored with what someone else has that we fail to see what God has given us and what the possibilities are for having a happy, meaningful life. I'll admit it's a challenge, because we inherited Eve's eyes that desire the sensual and are dazzled by beauty, and we have Cain's eyes that tend to compare. In addition, most of us live in an environment where we are bombarded by advertisements and images that are seductive, influencing what we want. Consequently, we can be so drawn to something we may begin to think in terms of "if I only had that," as in "if I only had Naboth's vineyard." We conclude we can only be happy with her looks, her husband, her body, their house, their children. I could go on and on, but you get the idea. With this kind of thinking, you miss out on the blessings God has for *you*, and you're blinded to the potential in your situation. Instead, you have a disturbed heart.

As the intensity of your coveting grows, your inner turmoil may be evident in your face as Ahab's was. If someone looks at you and says, "What's wrong?" or "Why is your face so red?," maybe it's time to consider what's happening. Maybe it's a cue to ask: *Am I wanting something I shouldn't have? Or don't need? Am I failing to see what I do have?* Maybe it's time to pray, "God, what potential do you have for me right now, right where I am?" It is the right time if you want "a heart at peace" that "gives life to the body" (Proverbs 14:30 NIV).

QUESTIONS FOR GROWTH (1 KINGS 21:1-29):

1. What does Ahab's reaction to Naboth's refusal to sell or trade his property reveal about him? Is it the way a king would act?
2. Why didn't Ahab ask Jezebel what she was planning to do to give him Naboth's vineyard?
3. Which of the Ten Commandments did King Ahab violate? Which ones did Jezebel break for Ahab to finally get Naboth's vineyard?
4. Does a person actually have to throw stones to be guilty of committing murder?
5. How can we change our countenance? What did Jesus do on the Mountain of Transfiguration that brought about a change in his countenance (Luke 9:28–29)?
6. Ahab kept the property even though he repented. Do you think he went ahead with his vegetable garden? Sometimes, after we get what we want, we decide it's not as important to us as we thought it would be.
7. What does this incident show us about how God regards coveting?
8. How is Ahab's story similar to David's story? How are they different?
9. What does Jezebel's solution to Ahab's depression reveal about her? About her relationship with Ahab?
10. Knowing our emotions are often revealed by our faces and/or body language, should we work hard on hiding what we feel? Or work hard on understanding what we feel?
11. Realizing inner feelings may be outwardly evident, how might this help us in understanding, relating to and working with other people?

CHAPTER 10—ASAPH: TANGLED EMOTIONS

As far as I knew, no one could see I was experiencing pangs of jealousy like Jezebel could see Ahab's coveting. No one was present the night I threw the magazine across the room. Neither had I mentioned my feelings to anyone except for one brief conversation with my English-teacher-writer friend. Nothing outwardly indicated my heart was disturbed; that is, there wasn't until our small Sunday school class studied Psalm 73.

The author of this psalm was Asaph, a Levite and a chorister associated with the temple in Jerusalem. He had a keen eye and a sensitive spirit. As he observed people day after day, coming and going, he noticed two groups.

Group One. It was made up of good people—people who had clean or pure hearts. They were loyal to God and lived by his standards.

Group Two. It consisted of people who were "wicked" (73:3 KJV) and "foolish" (73:3 KJV). Another Bible translation called them "arrogant" (73:3 NIV). These people disregarded God and lived the way they wanted to live.

As Asaph observed these two groups, he noticed the foolish, wicked people were being rewarded, and the good people weren't. This went against what he believed. Asaph believed God was truly good to his people, to those who have pure hearts. He had held to this belief—thought it to be true—yet reality showed otherwise. The wicked were being rewarded and blessed! Here's how Asaph described what he was observing about the foolish, wicked people.

> They do not suffer pain;
>
> they are strong and healthy.
>
> They do not suffer as other people do;
>
> they do not have the troubles that others have.
>
> And so they wear pride like a necklace and violence like a robe;
>
> their hearts pour out evil,
>
> and their minds are busy with wicked schemes.
>
> They laugh at other people and speak of evil things;
>
> they are proud and make plans to oppress others.
>
> They speak evil of God in heaven
>
> and give arrogant orders to everyone on earth.
>
> They have plenty and are always getting more. (Psalm 73:4–9, 12)

The wicked who prospered were extremely arrogant about their achievements. They seemed to live trouble-free lives and have no worries at all. If that weren't bad enough, the wicked were drawing God's people away. They eagerly believed what the wicked people said.

Especially disturbing to Asaph was the wicked people's denial of God's awareness of their actions. They said, "God will not know; the Most High will not find out" (Psalm 73:11). They were so confident—or some might say cocky—they believed God was unaware of their behavior. They thought they could get by with anything.

When Asaph "tried to understand all this, it troubled [him] deeply" (73:16 NIV) His faith "was almost gone" (Psalm 73:2). And even worse, he started wanting what the wicked people had. He said "I 'nearly lost my foothold for I *envied* the arrogant when I saw the prosperity of the wicked" (73:2b–3 NIV, author's emphasis). To lose his foothold meant he was about to lose his faith because he was jealous of those taking pride in how well they were doing.

What he had believed his whole life was now in jeopardy. His efforts at living a good life had not been worthwhile. In vain, he had kept his heart pure. He despaired at the complacency and success of the wicked, and at the same time, he would have liked to have had some of what they were experiencing.

As our class studied Psalm 73, I looked around at those in attendance. We were all hard-working, trying-to-make-ends-meet people who were trying to grow a church and weren't making much progress. We faithfully served God in the best way we knew how. We put much effort into living the Christian life, and yet life was hard, and we saw little fruit from our effort. Suddenly, I interrupted the teacher. I said, "I can certainly understand the psalmist's feelings. Things always seem to go well for the wicked. They prosper. They become wealthy. Look at us. Here we are trying to make a living, keep our bills paid, hold our little church together, and we never even seem to get a break. I don't understand. We're trying to do what God wants. Why doesn't God bless us?"

No one said a word. I imagine they were too shocked by my outburst. It was so unlike me. By looking in their eyes, though, I could tell some felt the same way. They were too nice to say anything! They would never be given to expressing themselves so strongly because they were good people—good just like Asaph.

After an awkward silence, the teacher went on with the lesson. As he did, I asked myself, *Where did this outburst come from?* I lived a simple life and preferred it that way. I wasn't dazzled or impressed by the possessions of others, but here I was agreeing with the psalmist about the rich being more blessed and sharing in his resentment.

My husband, who was in the class, wondered too. On the way home, Bob said, "You expressed some really strong feelings in class today. What's going on?"

Truthfully, I didn't know. Was I losing my foothold like Asaph was? Was I losing confidence in God? Did my outburst have anything to do with the "pangs of jealousy" I had been experiencing? I was genuinely confused. Maybe it was time to do what Asaph did and seek out a sanctuary place.

The Power of Sanctuary

A sanctuary is a place of refuge, a safe place. The place can be a spot where you can be with God, a place where you can talk freely with him and listen to what he has to say without interruption. A sanctuary can be a haven where you can withdraw from the stress of life and be refreshed. It can be a place where you can examine your own thinking without interruption or judgment and come to insightful conclusions about your life.

We can have more than one place of sanctuary—a church at a certain time of day, a favorite spot by a lake, or a shady spot in your backyard. The site I most often use is my office. That's where I read, journal, pray, meditate, and ask questions early in the morning while the rest of the household sleeps.

The psalmist's sanctuary was probably the temple in Jerusalem. Something happened in his worship or in his Levitical service there that gave him insight and reassurance. There he came to understand—and to believe—that although the wicked prospered in the present, they would eventually be punished. God would cast them into destruction. God gave Asaph no exact timetable. The wicked might prosper for years; but still judgment would occur.

God would take care of the wicked (issue judgment) in his time. No concrete evidence was given to Asaph, just the assurance that God had arranged things so evil people would get what they deserved sooner or later. They would be held accountable and punished for their actions. As a result of his sanctuary experience, Asaph was transformed spiritually and emotionally. His faith and confidence were renewed.

My sanctuary experience didn't result in a quick recovery as Asaph's did, although his psalm may simply have been a summary of his transforming experience. When we read something that happened in the past, the solutions often seem simpler and faster than when we experience something similar in the present. My sanctuary experience took a while.

Sanctuary's Work

Early in the morning, alone in my office with a Bible, a pen, and a notebook, I asked the Holy Spirit to help me. I trusted him to "teach" me and "make" me "remember" (John 14:26), so I could figure out why my heart was disturbed.

I started by writing out thoughts as they came to me. I didn't try to evaluate them at first or make them sound respectable or holy. I attempted to describe what I was feeling and had been feeling. As I did, I tried to name those feelings. While this sounds simple, it wasn't, because as we have noted in this book, jealousy is often intertwined with other emotions. I call it entanglement. Alice Frying in her book, *Reshaping a Jealous Heart*, speaks of it as layers. She said, "Jealousy is almost always multilayered. Underneath the top layer, the raw feelings of jealousy, there will probably be several other thoughts and feelings."[1] There were in my case. I raked around inside, lifting layers, untangling emotions to get to the bottom of what was bothering me. What I discovered at the bottom surprised me. I was disappointed in God.

During my thirties and forties, I had expected to become one of God's spokespersons—someone who delivered his messages, someone who encouraged and inspired others and someone whose opinion counted. While I had done some of this—as many Christians do—I was not where I thought I should be.

During those years, I had believed as Asaph did that God rewarded goodness. If I served God faithfully and consistently, God would call me up to a place of success just as the wedding host called up the guest who sat in the lowest place in one of Jesus's parables: "When you are invited, go and sit in the lowest place, so that your host will come to you and say, 'Come on up, my friend, to a better place.' This will bring you honor" (Luke 14:10). One day, I had believed, God would invite me up to a better place—a place of success, but it hadn't happened. I hadn't received the reward I had expected.

God, it seemed to me, was rewarding other people near my age. They could afford things. They had carpet that wasn't threadbare. They could travel. They had possessions. They had impressive résumés. I worked part time at a branch campus for a small college, where there was no opportunity for advancement or even hope of a pay raise. I didn't see much hope for things to change either. As I looked ahead to a future past fifty, the terrain of life's landscape looked bleak.

While this newly gained insight was helpful, I also found it interesting on several fronts:

1. I had never written out any goals for my life (a goal whereby a person could measure success or failure), but this expectancy that God would reward me had been an ever-present undercurrent in my life. I marveled something like this could be hidden in my heart.
2. I had never been a person who cared about possessions other than having necessities, or valuing money beyond having enough to pay bills, so I was surprised to find myself jealous of others who had material things.
3. As gloomy as all this sounds, that a person could be disappointed in God, jealous of others, and pessimistic

about the future, the realization was instead, quite freeing. I was reminded of Jesus's words, "You will know the truth, and the truth will set you free" (John 8:32). The feelings had clogged up my inner space, and once I was aware of them, they melted away. Their power dissipated. I felt all clean on the inside. My sanctuary experience had done its work. Well, almost all of its work.

Because I felt free from the emotions that were occupying valuable inner space, stopping there would have bren tempting, thinking I had completely resolved the issue. I remembered, though, a lesson I had learned earlier in my life when dealing with depression. You have to do something to keep those same feelings from returning and bringing more with them. Jesus warned us about this in a story he told. It was about an evil spirit leaving a person, traveling around, looking for a place to rest. If the evil spirit can't find such a place, it says to itself, "I will go back to my house" (Luke 11:24). When it gets back, the house is clean and fixed up. Then the evil spirit goes out and brings home seven other evil spirits who are worse than he is. They come and live with him. Consequently, the person who swept his house clean is in worse shape than he was at the beginning!

I didn't want my heart to be in worse shape. I didn't want to go back to being jealous, resentful, sad, and pessimistic. Neither did I want to add more disturbing emotions. Rather, I wanted my relationship with God to be healthy and strong. I wanted to be able to exclaim with Asaph, "How wonderful to be near God ... and to proclaim all that he has done!" (Psalm 73:28). Evidently, I had more sanctuary work to do.

Questions for Growth (Psalm 73):

1. Have you had life experiences that caused you to question the goodness of God? What were those experiences?
2. Does the insight Asaph gained in the sanctuary satisfy you? Does his conclusion help strengthen your faith?
3. Where is your sanctuary? Where do you go to work out your feelings—find out what they are and why you are experiencing them?
4. Some commentators say Asaph's worship was what changed him. How can worship change us? Or change our understanding or interpretation of events?
5. At the end of his psalm, what does Asaph say he is determined to do? (73:28)
6. If you were rich and famous, would you have any problems or questions about God being preferential to one group? Or is this something only those with less would question?
7. What is a foothold? And what are you doing to maintain yours?
8. Did God change the rich people or did he change Asaph to bring about a heart at peace? Who or what changed?

CHAPTER 11—DANIEL'S CRITICS: THERE'S ALWAYS SOMEONE BETTER

Many of us are in positions where performance counts and where we are assessed in terms of how others are doing. This could be in sales, sports, entertainment, teaching, weight, ministry, missions, or any number of other things. As a result, you may become conscious of those who outshine you and who receive recognition.

For example, you may have thought you had a solid place at work until someone younger was hired (or someone older). As you move around the office, you overhear comments about how well the new person is doing. You hear the boss say, "We've never had anybody here who could do graphics as well as you." And when you hear, "You add so much to our work force," you do a slow burn as your place is being usurped.

A comparison may occur when we evaluate what we do in terms of numbers. You started a Bible study, and then, the women's ministry director organized another class. Hers quickly grew and surpassed yours in attendance. You wonder how it could happen. You thought you were doing everything right, so why is she the one succeeding? The discrepancy is hard to take, especially when you hear the director say, "We've never had a Bible study leader like her. She is phenomenal."

In situations like these, we may begrudge the existence of those ahead of us. We'd like to see them fall off the pedestal everyone has them on. We might even want to "help" them fall off like those who were critical of Daniel.

If anyone deserved to be on a pedestal, it was Daniel. He had been taken captive as a young man in Jerusalem along with several others and forced to live in a foreign place. He did well. In fact, he thrived. He became known in his new home for his "good sense, knowledge, and wisdom" (Daniel 5:11).

Daniel's wisdom was helpful when King Belshazzar had an unusual experience. He saw a human hand writing on the wall of the palace. This frightened him. Daniel relieved the king's fears by explaining what the mysterious handwriting meant. The king was so pleased he honored Daniel. Belshazzar ordered his servants to dress Daniel in a robe of royal purple and to hang a gold chain of honor around his neck. He made Daniel the third in power in the kingdom.

That same night, King Belshazzar was killed, and Darius the Mede seized the throne. He immediately organized the kingdom under three administrators or supervisors. He appointed Daniel to serve as one of the three. Each administrator was responsible for a hundred twenty satraps or governors. The administrators were to look after the king's interests and supervise the satraps.

Daniel quickly emerged as the king's favorite administrator because he "showed that he could do better work than the other supervisors or the governors" (Daniel 6:3). Daniel "was so outstanding, the king considered putting him in charge of the whole empire" (6:3).

When the other administrators and the governors heard about this, they didn't like what they heard—perhaps because Daniel was still considered a foreigner. Even though it had been many years since he was taken from his homeland, his critics referred to him as "one of the exiles from Judah" (Daniel 6:13). They didn't think a person who wasn't native born should have a favored position in the kingdom.

Or maybe it bothered them because Daniel was so good. Too good. People sometimes resent those who are good. They believe it makes them look bad. If Daniel's critics could prove Daniel was flawed, that would make them look better.

Whatever the reason, the satraps along with the other two supervisors hated him. Day in and day out, they spied on Daniel. They hoped to discover some error in judgment, some special favor given to his own people (the Jews), or some mistake, so they could report him to King Darius and get Daniel in trouble.

They couldn't find anything "because Daniel was reliable and did not do anything wrong or dishonest" (Daniel 6:4). They were forced to conclude their efforts were useless unless they could accuse him of something connected with his religion. Perhaps something that would be a sign of disloyalty to the king. Ah, that just might work!

They said to King Darius, "Give orders that for thirty days no one be permitted to request anything from any god or from any man except from Your Majesty. Anyone who violates this order is to be thrown into a pit filled with lions" (Daniel 6:7). Perhaps it was their putting him on level with being a god that prompted King Darius to readily agree. He signed the law. Once he did this, the ban could not be undone. According to the laws of their land, the king could not abolish a law once it had been signed. The critics now were certain the object of their resentment would be eliminated.

When we experience feelings of jealousy or envy regarding someone who is better than we are, we may be *tempted* like Daniel's critics to undermine him or her. I doubt that any of us are going to do anything as extreme as getting a law passed to achieve this, but we do have ways of discrediting those who are superior to us. Here are some ways we can do that.

- We might gloat about our own achievements to try to build ourselves up in the eyes of those doing the evaluating.

- Our disgruntlement may surface as cattiness or as nasty, unkind words. We may do this in the person's presence or behind their back.
- We might slyly insert a negative comment into a conversation about the superior person to cast doubt about his character or her efficiency.
- We might hear something about them, something we know is untrue, and not speak up and make a correction. We also might repeat this to others who know her or work with him.
- We could even go so far as build a case about what the superior person is trying to achieve and get others to agree on a plan to sabotage his or her work.

Doing something like this, though, may backfire just as the effort of Daniel's critics did.

What They Hadn't Counted On

They were confident Daniel would disobey the king's decree. Sure enough, he went home, and there, just as he had always done, he knelt at the open windows facing toward his homeland and prayed to God. As they watched, they said, "Aha, now we've got him."

With that evidence, they hurried to the king. They said to him, "Daniel ... does not respect Your Majesty or obey the order you issued. He prays regularly three times a day'" (Daniel 6:13). What an indictment. Admirable in our eyes, but reason for punishment in the king's eyes. An order is an order, so Daniel was thrown into the lions' den.

God protected Daniel, something the king and his accusers hadn't expected. Daniel survived unscathed. When King Darius discovered this, he realized he had been manipulated. He gave orders to arrest all who had accused Daniel. He had them thrown together with their wives and children into the lions' den, where they were immediately devoured.

Our efforts at discrediting someone who arouses jealousy or envy in us may backfire, too.

We may lose value in the sight of others. Others may lower their opinion of us if we berate those we see as superior to us. When we talk about them, subtly or not so subtly, we may lose the respect of our peers, our coworkers, our boss, or our fellow believers.

We may become less efficient or less productive. If our focus is on the person we're jealous of, our ability to concentrate on a task may be affected. We might get the job done, but not as effectively as we would if we could fully give ourselves to the task at hand.

Our heart is disturbed. Being jealous or envious and figuring out ways to undermine the person who is more proficient than we are increases spiritual and emotional turmoil. The inner agitation we experience keeps peace from reigning and interferes with having a harmonious relationship with God.

So how can we keep from being like Daniel's critics? What can we do to deal with our jealous or envious feelings regarding those who appear more capable or talented than we are? Here are some suggestions:

Learn from the person. That person who is a cut above may be that way because of natural attributes or certain advantages or privileges because of their heritage, but it could also be because of choices they've made. They've had experiences we might be able to learn from.

At one time, I had a Daniel in my life—not that she was thrown to the lions. But like Daniel, she was well respected and wise. She was also good, kind, righteous, smart, generous and attractive. But what bothered me about her was life always appeared so easy for her. Not a ruffled feather or a misstep ever in sight. I often muttered to myself, "She sure has it easy," and "Everything always seems effortless for her." My life seemed so hard in comparison.

Then I had an opportunity to spend several days with her. As I got to know her better, I learned she was a highly disciplined person. While she had some advantages because of her heritage, she had made the most of her life because of what she asked of herself. Her self-discipline wasn't effortless. I returned home inspired. I became more disciplined, and I stopped saying, "She sure has it easy."

Dare to be average. This piece of advice isn't original with me. I ran across this while researching for another book. When I saw it, I chuckled and breathed a sigh of relief. I thought, *How refreshing*. We're always being told we are destined for greatness, or "you can be anything you want to be." The pressure is on us wherever we look. Articles pop up on the internet that hold "the secrets" for being accomplished. In three or four easy steps, we can be successful. But the truth is we can try, but there are no guarantees. We can, though, be average, even below average, and have a less pressured life. We can still serve God and experience the abundant life Jesus promised. We don't have to be king of the hill, valedictorian of the class, make the highest salary, always be the top salesperson or give the best speech. We can enjoy life right where we are.

To accept ourselves as average or below average doesn't mean we stop giving of our best to the Master. It doesn't mean we cease trying to improve ourselves. Growth is vital to the human spirit, but it does mean we stop wasting valuable time comparing ourselves with people we see as superior. Instead, we can be content with who we are.

Ask, "How can I help?" Harvest the energy involved in fretting about someone who is superior and use it for good. When James and John wanted to be "top dogs" in the kingdom Jesus was building, the other ten disciples "became angry with the two brothers" (Matthew 20:24). Recognizing the tension among them, Jesus got tough. He said, "If one of you wants to be great, you must be the servant of the rest" (Matthew 20:26).

To think and to act in terms of serving others is so much better in the long run than stewing about someone's superiority and harboring resentment. Serving takes the focus off self, decreases our tendency to compare ourselves with others, gives us opportunities to accomplish a lot of good in the world, allows us to experience personal growth, and most importantly, helps us maintain a heart at peace.

Find your identity in Christ. Some of my acquaintances have handled their feelings about being compared with others—whether they do it or someone else does and you hear about it—by allowing Christ to live in and through them. This principle is based on Philippians 1:21 where Paul says, "For me to live is Christ" (KJV). One acquaintance who uses this approach says, "I have been crucified with him, and the life I live is Jesus's life in me. And that's my identity. I am his and he is mine. This makes my heart sing and makes comparisons to others fade. I truly have everything I need for a meaningful life and a peaceful heart."

You'll probably notice a difference in the spirituality of these suggestions. For example, finding your identity in Christ and accepting yourself as average seem miles apart. I include them both plus the others because we are all at different places in our lives and in our spiritual strength. I try to include various ways to change our feelings so each person can latch on to a suggestion that speaks to them, not only here, but also in other chapters in this book. It's a matter of picking and choosing what says to us, "Yes, I can do this."

We need to know these ways because there will always be someone who outstrips us in every way. From time to time a Daniel, or Daniels, will be present in our lives. When that happens, we need to remember there are ways we can handle our reactions. We don't have to be jealous or envious. Instead we can ask ourselves, will we use what we know? Will we work at maintaining a peaceful heart while appreciating who we are?

QUESTIONS FOR GROWTH (DANIEL 6:1–27):

1. Why do you think King Darius agreed to the plot of the two supervisors, the governors, and others?
2. How many were jealous or envious of Daniel to the point of trying to get him in trouble? (6:7a)
3. What might we miss out on in life if our focus is on people we perceive to be better than us?
4. Why would someone's goodness or impeccable behavior cause someone else to be jealous or envious? What could possibly be going on in the mind of the other person? What kind of thoughts might he or she have?
5. What kind of person gets jealous of someone because the other is good? Because they are a better athlete? Because they have a better sales record? Because she manages her weight better?
6. What does jealousy in response to being compared say about the person? What need or deficiency might this person have? If you find yourself in this position, what are some things you can do about your feelings rather than resort to trickery as Daniel's critics did?
7. What are some *cultural* values that might influence our perception of who is better than we are?
8. Have you ever had someone be jealous of you because you were superior? Because you had good grades? Because you were skinny? Because you seemed to have a life of ease? Because you were often the winner in competitions? How did you respond to their jealousy?
9. Daniel was good. Being good is important, and as Christians, we are to be good, but what kind of reaction might this cause in other people? Should we stop being good so no one will be jealous of us? Would that solve the problem?

10. Daniel was probably at least seventy years old at the time he was falsely accused. Do you think age made it easier or harder for Daniel to be a righteous person?

CHAPTER 12—FEARFUL JEWS: WHEN IT'S US VS. THEM

Have you ever noticed how we live out our lives in groups of various kinds?

- Families
- Churches
- Organizations
- Businesses
- Ministries
- Friendship circles
- Mission groups
- Political parties

These are such broad, general categories that you may be better able to appreciate this observation by being more specific:

- A ministry group
- A missions group
- Your local church
- Your homeschoolers group
- Your knitting group or an exercise group
- A work project team

Groups like these (and there are many more) provide structure and support for our lives. They give us avenues through which to work, to play, to learn, to achieve, to worship, and to serve.

Dividing lines for some groups are fluid—that is, we can easily move in and out of them. Others are shaped by specific membership requirements. However, when the lines are formed, what often happens is that we start thinking in terms of "my group" and the "other group." This is normal—a matter of establishing identity. What may follow is the development of a sense of competition. At this point, the situation is ripe for growing group jealousy. It's not a given, but the Bible shows us that it does happen.

1. When John the Baptist preached, many flocked to the countryside to hear him. He urged people to repent of their sins because the kingdom of heaven was near. John urged people to show they were prepared by being baptized. One of the people John baptized was Jesus. Afterwards, Jesus launched his own ministry. Jesus drew an audience, too, and his disciples baptized as well. John's disciples noticed this and reported it to John. They said to him, "Teacher, you remember ... the one you spoke about? Well, he is baptizing now, and everyone is going to him!" (John 3:26).
2. As Jesus continued to preach, his following grew. It wasn't an organized movement (the lines were fluid) but was a recognizable group. It sparked fear into the lives of Jews who worshiped the God of Abraham, Isaac, and Jacob and who tried to live by the Law of Moses. They valued their faith, their traditions, and their way of doing things.
3. Jesus, in what he taught and what he did, challenged their values. At least, the Jews perceived it this way. They worried his *followship* would continue to grow, so some Jewish leaders maneuvered to get Jesus tried before Pilate, the local Roman authority. The leaders thought their motive was pure, that they were right to

oppose Jesus and get him eliminated, but Pilate didn't see their effort as righteous. He said the Jewish leaders did what they did "because they were jealous" (Matthew 27:18 and Mark 15:10).

4. Later, as Paul preached in many places throughout the Roman Empire, more people became followers of Jesus, sparking jealousy among the Jews again. For example, when Paul was in Antioch of Pisidia, "nearly everyone in the town came to hear the word of the Lord. When the Jews saw the crowds, they were filled with jealousy" (Acts 13:44-45). When Paul was in Thessalonica, he was successful in winning many Jews and Greeks to the Christian faith. That was further cause for alarm. Not only was he convincing Jews to become Christ followers, but he was also winning Greeks. As a result, "some Jews were jealous" (Acts 17:5).

John's disciples, the Jews who had Jesus arrested, and those who opposed Paul were earnest people. All were being protective. As they saw what was occurring, they were jealous. We may be tempted to feel the same way when we notice differences between our group and another group. I know I've been tempted. My life has been—and is—very much involved with groups. What can we learn from these biblical examples that will help us understand our feelings when we are in an "us" versus "them" environment?

Biblical Insight

Numbers matter. While we like to think—and sometimes say—numbers don't matter, when it comes to evaluating groups, we often rely on numbers. Size becomes a measuring rod of success. If the "other group" has more members, we're tempted to wonder, does this mean they have something more attractive to offer? Does this mean something is wrong with us? Will they draw members away from our group?

Values are valued. The Jews who were jealous of Jesus and Paul saw Christ followers as challenging their history and their faith practices. Their jealous response was a protective one because they earnestly believed their way was the right way.

We may feel that way about a group in which we participate. Perhaps it was founded for a particular purpose, which is why being a part of the group is important to us. Maybe the group was formed in response to a biblical mandate, a particular calling from God, or from a recognized or perceived need. But suppose another group comes along and claims to be more biblical, how would you feel? Would this imply your group hadn't really heard from God? Or you hadn't understood your mission correctly?

Fear compounds. Jealousy in and of itself is a strong feeling, and fear makes it worse. Already worried about Jesus's power and *followship*, the Jews became terrified when Jesus brought Lazarus back to life. Something had to be done. The Pharisees and the chief priests met with their governing body, the Sanhedrin council. They said, "What shall we do? Look at all the miracles this man is performing! If we let him go on in this way, everyone will believe in him" (John 11:47–48). Everyone? That's a lot of people. They feared there wouldn't be any Jews left who believed in the God of Abraham, Isaac, and Jacob. From there, their fear escalated even more. Some of the leaders said, "The Roman authorities will take action and destroy our Temple and our nation!" (11:48).

When fear attaches itself to jealousy, our minds entertain exaggerated thoughts such as *Oh, no, everyone is going to join the 'other' group. We'll be left with no one. Our group is going to die.* As thoughts like these circulate over and over in our minds, we may feel an urgency to do something. The Jews who were jealous of Jesus did. From the time Lazarus was raised, "the Jewish authorities made plans to kill Jesus" (John 11:53). The chief priests and Pharisees even resorted to engaging false witnesses to bring about Jesus's death, ignoring their own standards of fairness.[1]

As the number of Christ followers increased, the Jews in Thessalonica tried to get rid of Paul. They "gathered worthless loafers from the streets and formed a mob. They set the whole city in an uproar and attacked the home" where Paul was staying (Acts 17:5). Fortunately, Paul, along with his traveling companion, Silas, was able to escape and move on to a new place to minister.

Now I doubt that anyone reading this book is going to manipulate someone's arrest or form a mob out of fearful jealousy. Having a thought like that would be enough to disturb your peace if it weren't already disturbed by your comparison and fear. What we might be more tempted to do is use words as weapons as the Jews in Antioch did when they were jealous of Paul.

Words as Weapons

The Jews in Antioch "disputed what Paul was saying and insulted him" (Acts 13:45). We can dispute with actual members of the "other" group or we can challenge what they stand for behind their backs. We may even question their values or goals, even feign genuine interest in order to reveal their flaws and weaknesses.

We can insult members of the "other" group face-to-face or talk about them to others. I recently was in a meeting where I heard a women's ministry leader describe the difference between women's ministries and a women's mission organization. She said women's ministries went all the way back to the Bible, but this particular women's mission organization started on a certain date in history. I immediately thought, *Wait a minute! Isn't she one-upping the missions organization? By linking women's ministries to the Bible, isn't she implying this group is the better group, the more spiritual of the two? Actually, to organize on a particular date in history doesn't make what you do less biblical. If it did, many Christian organizations would be suspect. Besides, what we know as women's ministry today came about during the latter part of the twentieth century. It doesn't have a direct, continuous line with what happened in the early church.* As thoughts like these flooded my mind, I had to say to myself, "Get a grip, Brenda. If you keep going like this, you're going to have heartburn. Don't you value a heart at peace?" I did—and I do, and that's why it's good to know some ways for dealing with group jealousy and even improving the situation.

Don't participate in or contribute to agitating chatter. I understand we may need to talk when we find ourselves being jealous of another group. We may need conversation to gain some emotional relief or to get someone else's take on the situation. What we must be careful about is getting into a jealousy-motivated conversation with other members of our group that makes the situation worse. Sometimes as we talk with other members of our group, exaggerating a little here or there about the other group, the conversation takes on a fun element. We actually enjoy putting the other group down. At the same time, we're keeping group differences alive and making the issues that separate us worse. This kind of chatter gets people riled up and doesn't solve anything. It does, though, make your heartburn worse.

Reevaluate your group. The jealousy that surfaces in an "us" versus "them" environment may indicate it's time to reassess your group. Any group can lose their motivation, become stagnant, or lose sight of their goals and/or their mission. One way to evaluate is by asking questions such as these: Are we on the right track? Is our initial purpose still relevant? Is this the best way we can serve God? To respond to a need? Has culture changed in such a way that we may need to re-think how we do things? Are our methods old-fashioned, or do they need new life breathed into them? Has our group lost its sensitivity to the leadership of the Holy Spirit? Asking questions like these can get us back on target, doing what our group values and doing it with renewed vigor.

Pray for the other group. Our jealousy of another group may be so strong we think of them as our enemies. Consequently, it might be wise to remember what Jesus said about our enemies. He said, "Love your enemies ... and pray for those who mistreat you" (Luke 6:27–28, also in Matthew 5:43–44).[2]

When you see members of the "other" group, inquire about how they are doing. Ask: How can I pray for you? What does your group currently need from God? Showing concern and praying will soften your heart, reduce jealousy's power, and perhaps change your thinking. We won't be quite so judgmental when we care enough to pray for those we regard as enemies.

Adopt Paul's attitude. Suppose the other group really is more talented. Or larger. Yet if you remain convinced your group and what it stands for is important, then work at keeping jealousy at bay by seeing group differences the way Paul did.

In many of the places in which Paul preached, he attracted crowds and won many converts, but his face-to-face audience decreased when he was put in prison. Now this could have been a time when Paul became envious—envious of preachers who were free to travel, free to attract large crowds. Instead, Paul saw his guards and occasional visitors as a group he could reach with the gospel. He saw his imprisonment as helping "the progress of the gospel" (Philippians 1:12), and it did. He was still able to make converts and help churches by writing letters.

We can still have meaningful group experiences and be effective even if our group is not the best, the largest, the most famous, the most spirited, or the most up-to-date. God works in small groups as well as in large groups. God works in obscure places just as he works in big prominent places. What matters is that we have eyes to see and hearts to serve. Even when others were jealous, quarrelsome, and preaching from a spirit of selfish ambition, Paul said, "It does not matter! I am happy about it—just so Christ is preached" (Philippians 1:18). This is the approach I took in response to the ministry leader who put down missionary women by linking ministry women with the Bible. I thanked God he was using her and her ministry. Women were being reached, and that's what mattered.

The Jews who zealously defended their group missed out on seeing God in action. His Son was in their midst, revealing God's love for them, providing them a way of forgiveness for their sins. Paul was God's person, bringing freshness to their faith, giving them a way to fulfill God's original purpose for them—to be a light to the nations. Through John the Baptist, Jesus, and Paul, God was making his love and forgiveness available to both Jews and Gentiles, but some didn't see it because fear and jealousy got in the way. Let's not let that happen to us. Let's look for what God is doing wherever we are—in whatever group we belong.

Questions for Growth (John 3:22–26, John 11:45–53, Acts 13:42–50, and Acts 17:1–9):

1. What groups do you belong to or are involved with? If you had to identify yourself in terms of the groups you are in, what would you say?
2. For what purpose were your groups organized? Why do they exist?
3. Why might it be important to consider what your motive is for belonging?
4. How do you recognize when a group feels threatened by another group?
5. How do you explain the fact that one Christian group could be jealous of another Christian group? If all the members are Christian, then how could they be jealous of others?
6. Which one of Eve's temptations is evident when one group is jealous of another group? Beauty, sensuality, or one-upmanship?
7. What might make a group leader fear being replaced? What might she observe that would cause her to be afraid of losing affection or her position?
8. Jealousy is often suspicious in nature. How might we check out a situation to see if our suspicions are accurate and worthy of concern?
9. Coveting is sometimes part of the dynamics in an "us" versus "them" situation. How could what others *have* affect our group? What kind of things might we covet?

CHAPTER 13—JOHN THE BAPTIST: MAKING HAPPINESS COMPLETE

When I was teaching a Sunday school class of mixed adults (young and old, male and female), one young woman in the class had several personal problems including a difficult marriage. I often spent time with Shelley,[1] listening to her, and praying for her. One Sunday when she wasn't in class, I wondered where she was. Afterward, on the way to morning worship, I ran into her in the hall. With a twinkle in my eye, I said, "You're late!" She said, "Oh, I went to the new class."

"New class?"

"Yeah, the one starting for young adults."

Remember that jealous flash we talked about earlier? Well, I had a jealous flash at that moment, and I let it show. "You what?!"

She seemed oblivious. "Yeah, I really liked it. I think I will go to that class from now on."

I mumbled something, excused myself, and headed for the auditorium. I was upset. I had invested so much time in her, and now she was leaving my class. I'm not proud of this moment. I tell this about myself so you can understand why I marvel at John the Baptist for not getting upset when his disciples reported a competing ministry. We looked briefly at this incident in the last chapter where we studied group jealousy, but now I want us to focus more on John himself.

Not that he was jealous! In fact, William Barclay, author of *The Daily Study Bible*, calls him "a man without envy."[2]

Why do I want us to look at John the Baptist then, if envy or jealousy wasn't a problem for him? Because I believe his answer to his disciples' jealousy offers us help with some of our heartburn issues. I'm convinced of this because his answer helped me.

The disciples' jealousy may have been triggered by an argument they had "about the matter of ritual washing" (John 3:25). The argument could have been with one other established Jew or with several. Perhaps one of them said something like this: "Well, you know your teacher's not the only one who baptizes. Jesus is ministering now, and people are being baptized by him."

This information disturbed John's disciples. They hurried to John and said, "Rabbi, you know the one who was with you on the other side of the Jordan? The one you authorized with your witness? Well, he's now competing with us. He's baptizing, too, and everyone's going to him instead of us.'"[3]

They didn't want their leader to be in second place, to lose out to someone else. They might have also been afraid people might stop following John altogether, and they wanted John to be as upset as they were. John could have reacted this way. He could have felt threatened by what his disciples reported. He could have been tempted to defend his status, but John didn't. Instead he said, "No one can have anything unless God gives it. You yourselves are my witnesses that I said, 'I am not the Messiah, but I have been sent ahead of him.' The bridegroom is the one to whom the bride belongs; but the bridegroom's friend, who stands by and listens, is glad when he hears the bridegroom's voice. This is how my own happiness is made complete. He must become more important while I become less important" (John 3:27–30). In his answer, I found insight and guidance for having a heart at peace.

John saw his life and his work as a gift from God as evidenced by his saying, "No one can have anything unless God gives it to him" (John 3:27). John was born to parents who were old. They probably didn't live long enough to see him to manhood. In the time they had with him, I'm sure they told him about what had been prophesied about him before he was born (see Luke 1:13–17). Any parent would have. Some kids would have felt pressured by something like this. John could have chafed against his destiny. Instead, he saw it as God's doing, as a gift.

We all come out of the womb with certain attributes, basics that influence who and what we are. We may not like some of those attributes we were born with. We may even blame them for keeping us from being who we would like to be. We wish we were different. If I didn't gain weight so easily, if I were taller, if I had a different nose, if I had a higher IQ, then I could be successful or admired. This kind of thinking makes us susceptible to being jealous, envious, or covetous. But what if we took another approach? What if we looked on our attributes as gifts from God and responded with thanksgiving? Expressing gratitude mellows the heart, offers us a different perspective, and raises our appreciation level, resulting in a more enjoyable and meaningful life.

John knew who he was, or perhaps I should say he knew who he was *not*. He reminded his disciples they had heard him say, "I am *not* the Messiah" (John 3:28, author's emphasis) whom the people were expecting. On another occasion, John insisted he was *not* Elijah and *not* the Prophet, two other people the Jews thought might appear (see John 1:21). Many people thought John could be any one of these three (the Messiah, Elijah, or the Prophet) because of the large crowds that gathered to hear him. John, though, insisted, he was *not* any of these three persons. Men less certain of their identity might be tempted to play it for all it was worth. John, though, was not "a blade of grass bending in the wind," being one way one day and another way at another time (Luke 7:24). John was his own person, confident in who he was, which was evident in several ways.

- The way he dressed: He "wore clothes made of camel's hair, with a leather belt around his waist" (Mark 1:6) which wasn't normal attire.
- His diet: "His food was locusts and wild honey" (Mark 1:6).
- His style of preaching: He spared no one in calling out their sins, even calling some listeners vipers or snakes (see Luke 3: 7–14).
- His message was never diluted or compromised by who was in the crowd listening.

Knowing who he was and who he was not made John stronger as a person, and it can do the same for us. Knowing who we are strengthens us so we are not so susceptible to the comparing and competing that figures so strongly in being jealous, envious, or covetous. We are also less likely to give in to social pressure when we're feeling forced to act and to believe in a certain way. When we know what we value, we are less apt to be taken in by the allure of what we see in others or what society applauds. We can be our own person.

John knew what his role was, and he never stepped outside that role. He was "sent ahead of" Jesus (John 3:28) to prepare the way for him. I like to think of him as "the warm-up act"—getting people ready to receive the main feature. To help his disciples understand, John explained his role was like being the friend of a bridegroom. In their culture, the friend of the bridegroom arranged the wedding, invited the guests, and presided at the wedding feast. He brought the bride and the bridegroom together, and he guarded the bridal chamber so no false lover could get in. He would only open the door when he heard the bridegroom's voice. When he recognized the bridegroom's voice, he rejoiced, and let him in. His job was done, and he willingly faded out of the scene, something John was willing to do now that Jesus was connecting with God's people, the Jews. John didn't have a "*Do I have to*?" attitude. He gladly fulfilled his role as he stood by and listened for the bridegroom's voice that would indicate his work was completed.

Knowing what my role was to be was of particular importance to me as I emerged from discerning what was behind my "pangs of jealousy." My primary role through the years had been that of a homemaker—a role that would change somewhat now that my youngest child was leaving home. With the nest empty, I envisioned myself as keeping the home fires burning, so as my sons traveled the world, they would always have a welcoming place available to return whenever they wanted to or needed to. But the other role—that of being a Christian communicator—was what I was concerned about. Should I continue? If I did, was there a way I could do it gladly, without fear of failing or possibly being disappointed in God again?

I answered these questions in much the same way I did when I uncovered what was behind my "pangs of jealousy"—by using sanctuary time—writing in my journal, meditating on Scripture, and verbalizing my thoughts to God. I also talked with Bob, my husband, and Pat, my English teacher-writer-friend. I asked them, "How do you see me?" They both acknowledged I was a student of the Bible who felt compelled to share what she learned. Pat called it sharing wisdom with practical application. Bob said, "You've got to share God's Word. It's like a fire burning within you."[4] If their observations were correct, then my pursuit to be a writer, a teacher, and a speaker in life's first half made sense. Perhaps my role didn't need to change for life's second half as much as I needed to change. This meant not worrying about being a success or failure. I needed to be more committed, not a blade of grass waving in the breeze, being one thing one day, and then trying something else, so I gave new effort to what I was doing by setting goals, at first for a few years out. When those goals were completed, I started setting goals each year. I don't always meet my goals, but here's the thing: they keep me focused so I'm not looking to my right and to my left, comparing myself, measuring myself in terms of what others are doing. Well, mostly. Sometimes I have to pull myself back in, like the day I was jealous because Shelley was leaving my class.

I couldn't get her and my reaction off my mind as I sat in church. I didn't hear much of what the minister said, but I heard John's answer to the disciples loud and clear. As he explained to them the role he had, the role that was prophesied before he was born, that one he had fulfilled gladly, he also said, "This is how my own happiness is made complete. He must become more important while I become less important" (John 3:29–30).

Sitting there, ruminating over my reaction, I asked myself, did I want complete happiness? In a way I was happy. If anyone had tapped me on the shoulder at that moment, while I was "listening" to the sermon, and said, "Are you happy?" I would have said, "Yes, of course." But I wasn't completely happy, because jealousy and fuming were taking up valuable inner space. Envy, coveting, and some of their cousins can do the same thing. Other emotions can also disturb the heart, and so does sin. That's why, if we want complete happiness, we need to do what John did: allow Jesus to increase while we decrease.

Reluctantly, I asked myself, *Is my jealous reaction going to increase Jesus*? No, I realized it wasn't. Would Shelley's going to another class? Yes, perhaps it would. It might be better for Shelley at this stage of her life to be involved in a class with her peers. It might help her grow spiritually and solve some of her problems. I found her after the worship service and said to her, "I'm sorry for my reaction. You're doing the right thing."

She looked surprised. "Really?"

"Yes, I think this new class will be a blessing to you." We both smiled and hugged each other. As I walked away, I thought, perhaps in a way I was a "warm-up act" for Shelley. Our meeting together, our many conversations, and her being in my class provided a spiritual readiness that might provide fertile soil for spiritual growth in a new class. Whether she grew or not, I knew I was growing. I learned several things from John the Baptist's answer to his disciples' concern over the competition, but the most important thing I learned is if we want our happiness to be complete, Jesus must increase while we decrease.

Questions for Growth (John 3:22–30):

1. What kind of reaction do you think John's disciples wanted from him when they reported to him what they had heard about Jesus baptizing?
2. Who are you? Can you describe yourself in terms of "I am" using nouns/roles? Or say what you are not as John did when he said, "I am not the Messiah," "I am not Elijah," and "I am not the Prophet"?
3. What do you think would have been the reception of Jesus if John the Baptist hadn't prepared the way? Why was it important that the people be prepared?
4. John's purpose was preparing the way for Jesus. What has God called you to do? What is your purpose?
5. What is the point of John's illustration about the bride and bridegroom?
6. What does John's response to his disciples tell you about him?
7. How do you express the role and place of Jesus in your life?
8. What is incomplete happiness?
9. Does John's playing the lesser role mean that all believers should aspire for lesser roles?
10. What if every Christian had John's mind-set, that Jesus must increase and he must decrease? What difference, if any, would that make in the lives of believers?
11. John's response to his disciples' concern was not a limp response or self-deprecating. This was real humility. How do you define humility? Is this something a Christian can or should develop in his or her life? What would humility look like in the life of a believer?
12. What's the difference in how King Saul saw his role as the first king of Israel and how John the Baptist saw his

role as the forerunner of Jesus?

13. What rewards might a person playing a secondary role or doing a subordinate task receive?

CHAPTER 14—SIMON MAGUS: RIGHTING THE HEART

When is the best time to deal with feelings of jealousy, envy, or coveting? R. T. Kendall in his book, *Jealousy—The Sin No One Talks About: How to Overcome Envy and Live a Life of Freedom*, says, "Do not play around with jealousy. Don't deny it. Admit to it ... if you do not nip jealousy in the bud, its end will be a destruction you don't want to contemplate."[1] He says we should immediately go to our knees, pour out our complaint to the Lord, and confess our feelings. The sooner we deal with our feelings, the better off we will be. The longer we hold on to them, the feelings will grow, increase in strength, take up valuable inner space, and complicate our lives. Like Simon Magus, we may end up with a severe case of heartburn.

Simon Who?

The Bible tells of several Simons. Simon Magus is one we hear little about, but I find him fascinating. He was a magician, some say sorcerer, who lived in the city of Samaria. For a long time, he had astounded Samaritans with his magic. He may have had an exaggerated sense of self because he claimed he was a great man. Many Samaritans felt the same way about him. Everyone in the city, from all classes of society, paid close attention to him. About him, they said, "He is that power of God known as 'The Great Power'" (Acts 8:10). This didn't mean they were thinking of him as being spiritually powerful in the Christian sense—like we might think of someone like Billy Graham. Simon Magus had unusual powers that baffled the Samaritans; they could see no other explanation for what he did except that his power must come from God.

When Philip, one of the seven men chosen to help distribute food to widows in Jerusalem, went to Samaria, he also captured the people's attention. He shared "the good news of the Kingdom of God" and talked "about Jesus Christ" (Acts 8:12). Through Philip, many miracles occurred. "Evil spirits came out from many people ... and many paralyzed and lame people were healed" (8:7). Many also believed in Jesus and were baptized when they heard about him. Simon was one of them. After being baptized, Simon stayed close to Philip and watched in awe the wonders he performed.

Meanwhile, back in Jerusalem, the apostles "heard that the people of Samaria had received the word of God" (Acts 8:14). They found this a little hard to believe since they had little respect for Samaritans, so they sent Peter and John to check out the situation.

When they arrived, Peter and John found that the Samaritans were indeed believers; however, there was a problem. The believers "had only been baptized in the name of the Lord Jesus" (Acts 8:16). There was no visible manifestation of the Holy Spirit, so Peter and John prayed for them. They "placed their hands on them, and they received the Holy Spirit" (8:17).

They received the Holy Spirit in such a way that Simon was impressed—not with what was happening to the people but with Peter's and John's power. When they laid hands on the people, something extraordinary—something visible—happened. Exactly what Simon saw, we don't know. What we do know is Simon was impressed, and he *wanted* what he saw. If he could do with his hands what Peter and John did, then he would be admired even more. He didn't give this as the reason when he offered to buy the power. He gave a more noble reason. He said he wanted the gift "so that anyone I place my hands on will receive the Holy Spirit" (Acts 8:19).

That's when we hear from another Simon—Simon Peter. Peter immediately responded with his version of nip it in the bud. He said, "May you and your money go to hell, for thinking that you can buy God's gift with money!" (Acts 8:20). The very idea was outrageous. Spiritual power wasn't something you could buy. Simon's heart was "not right in God's sight" (8:21). Indeed, several things were wrong.

His motive. Simon didn't want spiritual power to help others as Peter, John, and Philip were doing. He wanted to enhance his own reputation and exalt himself, to be someone greater than he already was. Peter called it an "evil plan" (Acts 8:22).

His method. Simon Magus regarded spiritual power as a commodity that could be purchased with money. While he may have professed faith under Philip's preaching, his offer to buy it showed his lack of awareness of how God works and what God wants. He didn't know that spiritual power was—and is—a gift from God. He only knew he *wanted* what he saw and figured money was the way to get it. Doesn't everyone respond to money?

His envy. Wanting to be like Peter and John wasn't Simon's first experience of being envious. Peter said he was "full of bitter envy" (Acts 8:23). Time and time again, he had envied, and his feelings had taken on a bitter quality because in his pursuits to be great, he never quite got what he was looking for. His inner needs were never met. Consequently, his resentment built up. The combination of envy and resentment took up an enormous amount of room, making his heart full.

His bondage. Do you remember what God said to Cain when he wanted what his brother had? God said, "Sin is crouching at your door. It wants to rule you, but you must overcome it" (Genesis 4:7). That's what was happening to Simon Magus. His bitter envy held him hostage, making him a "prisoner of sin" (8:23). Simon was a prisoner to his desire to have more, to be acclaimed more and more by others. This desire overwhelmed him and controlled him.

Peter had a solution for Simon Magus—a way for making his heart right. He said, "Repent, then, of this evil plan of yours, and pray to the Lord that he will forgive you for thinking such a thing" (Acts 8:22). We all need to repent and pray at times if we want to have inner peace and be spiritually strong.

Repent and Pray

To repent means confessing our wrong feelings, thoughts, and actions, being sorry or remorseful, and having a desire to change. Peter urged Simon to do this in prayer, asking God for forgiveness. For me, this means verbalized prayer; that is, confessing out loud, expressing remorse, asking God to forgive me and to help me do better. While I realize silent praying can and does accomplish this for many people, praying in my thoughts doesn't achieve release and freedom for me. I need to pray out loud. Even when I write in my journal what I am confessing and express my sorrow there, I still need to speak out loud to God. You may not need to do a verbal prayer when you repent; there is no set way. What is needed is genuine repentance and asking God's forgiveness.

Repentance and prayer cleanse the heart, refresh the spirit and help us move forward with renewed energy and strength. This is something Carey Nieuwhof, pastor, author, in-demand speaker and leadership expert, experienced when he was jealous of another leader. He became convicted of his need to repent when reading this passage from the book of James.

> Are there any of you who are wise and understanding? You are to prove it by your good life, by your good deeds performed with humility and wisdom. But if in your heart

> you are *jealous, bitter*, and selfish, don't sin against the truth by boasting of your wisdom. Such wisdom does not come down from heaven; it belongs to the world, it is unspiritual and demonic ... But the wisdom from above is ... peaceful, gentle, and friendly. (James 3:13–7, author's emphasis)

In his book, *Didn't See It Coming*, Nieuwhof said when he read this passage, he realized it described him. He said, "I felt jealous of another leader I suspected was a better speaker than I was. I had allowed it to eat me up. I felt selfish, insecure and did *not* want to share the spotlight any more than I had to. Pride grew ugly things in my heart, things that were not from God at all. They were the opposite of what God offers.

"Instead of blowing the passage off and ignoring it, I admitted that it described me. I confessed it. I didn't want those words to characterize me."[2] The next day he read the James passage again, praying as he did. It took a week of reading and praying every day until Nieuwhof felt forgiven, and jealousy relinquished its grip on his heart.

Being honest and praying every day for a week—or even longer—lets us know that "righting the heart" isn't always simple or easy. In fact, some of us may need others to help us, especially if our feelings are as entrenched as Simon's were.

The Power of Confession

Maybe it was the forcefulness of Peter's words that prompted Simon to ask him and John for help. He said, "Please pray to the Lord for me" (Acts 8:24). Or perhaps it was the jolt of having someone else see what was in his heart—something he had camouflaged—that prompted Simon's request. Or maybe it was Peter's suggestion that it might not be possible for him to be forgiven. When Peter told Simon how to right his heart, he said, "Pray to the Lord that, *if possible*, the intent of your heart may be forgiven you" (Acts 8:22 NRSV, author's emphasis). Regardless of the reason, Simon wilted and asked Peter and John to pray for him.

We, too, may feel the same way at times when we are trying to nip jealousy, envy or coveting in the bud. We just can't seem to do it by ourselves, even though we know it needs to be done. Perhaps that's why James, the author of the biblical passage that convicted Carey Nieuwhof, said, "Confess your sins to one another and pray for one another, so that you will be healed" (James 5:16). The person you confess to could be a friend, a fellow church member, a pastor, or a professional counselor—anyone as long as it is someone who is trustworthy, listens well, and prays earnestly.

Admittingly, confessing our faults to someone takes courage, yet admitting to what we are dealing with and praying with someone can be very beneficial.

- Confessing your feelings to someone gets them out in the open where you can see them more clearly and consider them more objectively. They will lose some of their power over you as your inner space is being freed up.
- Another person may help you sort out your feelings. As we have seen, jealousy, envy, and covetousness can be accompanied by other emotions such as fear, malice, anger, resentment, and even hatred. In your heart, these feelings swirl around, agitating your spirit, but a listener can help you name your feelings and gain some control over them.
- Another person can pray for you, and as they pray, you may find you are able to pray when you thought you couldn't. The other person's prayer—and their expressed faith—may give you courage and help you know how to articulate what is in your heart.

- Another person's listening, eye contact, and praying can reassure us that what the Scripture tells us is true: "If we confess our sins to God, he will keep his promise and do what is right: he will forgive us our sins and purify us from all our wrongdoing" (1 John 1:9).

Whether we repent and pray alone or in the presence of someone else, admitting our guilt and asking God to forgive us frees up our inner space and gives God the channel he needs to come in, fill our hearts with peace, and strengthen us for the days ahead. This is true whether our sin is fresh (when we can more easily nip it in the bud), whether it's been around a long time (and we've become a prisoner of sin), or somewhere in between. Wherever we are, the combination of repentance and prayer is an effective way to right our hearts.

The Bible doesn't tell us what happened after Simon Magus asked Peter and John to pray for him. Did they do what he asked? Was Simon's heart righted? Did he learn from what Peter told him? How did his story end? I don't know, but I do know this. I know how I want my story to end. I want it to conclude with "Brenda Poinsett learned to pray and to seek forgiveness when feelings of jealousy, envy, or coveting entered her heart. She learned to nip the feeling in the bud and have a heart at peace." I hope your story ends the same way.

Questions for Growth (Acts 8:4–25):

1. How would Peter have known about Simon's envy and sin?
2. How would you define bitter envy?
3. What is a prisoner of sin? How does one become a prisoner of sin?
4. Why is it hard to admit sin?
5. John the Baptist was a man without envy, and Simon Magus was full of bitter envy. What might explain the difference?
6. How might envy of the power of another Christian affect a person's faith walk?
7. What are some gifts spiritual leaders have that money cannot buy? How did they get those gifts? What might it say about us if we envy them or desperately want their gifts?
8. If you can't buy spiritual power, how do you attain it?
9. Why is exaltation of self a temptation for preachers, teachers, speakers, actors, magicians and such?
10. How might jealousy, bitterness and selfishness in your heart keep you from being wise and understanding (see James 3:13–18)?
11. Why do we need to be honest with ourselves and with God? Why is honesty important to having a heart at peace?

CHAPTER 15—PAUL AND THE GALATIANS: LETTING THE SPIRIT DIRECT

In the biblical examples we've looked at in this book, we've learned much about *wanting* and the nature of jealousy, envy, and coveting. We understand how damaging these emotions and some of their cousins can be. We discovered various tools we can use to deal with these feelings. We specifically learned the importance of nipping feelings in the bud through repentance, confession, and prayer, but we don't always nip when we should or use the tools we're aware of. We hesitate and let the problems grow.

In addition, as we move along in life, we encounter territory we haven't traversed before—territory that presents new challenges such as I was experiencing at midlife. Consequently, we may not recognize jealousy, envy, or coveting or deal with these feelings in a timely fashion. You would think we would, but feelings can be deceptive. That's why we need to be aware of more help to assist us over the long haul. This help is available to us through the Holy Spirit. He speaks to us, helps us know what's right, calls things into remembrance and convicts us when we are wrong. That's why Paul advised believers in Galatia to "Let the Spirit direct" (Galatians 5:16).

Another Example of "Us" Versus "Them"

Strong emotions were getting the best of Galatian believers even though they knew better. At the heart of the matter was that sides had developed among them over differences in beliefs. One group believed a person was put right with God by faith in Jesus Christ. By faith alone, they insisted, their sins were forgiven and a relationship with him had begun. The other group agreed with the importance of faith, but they said a person also needed to keep Jewish laws in order to be put right with God. Each side was adamant about their position which resulted in strife and discord among them. Of them, Paul said, they "become enemies and they fight; they become *jealous*, *angry*, and *ambitious*. They separate into parties and groups; they are *envious*, get drunk, have orgies, and do other things like these" (Galatians 5:20–21, author's italics). There were other characteristics besides these, but we are particularly interested in jealousy, envy, hatred, anger, and ambition because they relate to the heartburn we've been exploring in this book.

Paul was both distressed and concerned about their behavior. He said, "that those who live like this will not inherit the kingdom of God" (Galatians 5:21 NIV). The kingdom of God is not a geographical location. It is where God rules and reigns—a place where believers can flourish and spiritual fruit be produced, fruit such as "love, joy, peace, patience, kindness, goodness, faithfulness, humility, and self-control" (Galatians 5:22–23).

I want to be in this kingdom, don't you? I want to be in a place where I can flourish and spiritual fruit be produced. As you know, from what I've previously written, I'm particularly interested in the fruit of peace and having a purposeful life.

What did Paul say Christians should do if they want to move from a lifestyle of jealousy, complaining, competitiveness, and envy to being people who are joyful, loving, peaceful and self-controlled? He said, "Let the Spirit direct your lives" (Galatians 5:16).

WAIT A MINUTE!

The people Paul was writing to were believers, so wasn't the Spirit already directing their lives? Isn't this his role? Doesn't he become our spiritual director when we become believers?

Yes, the Holy Spirit does, but his leadership is challenged from time to time by what the Bible calls our "human nature" (GNT) or "flesh" (NIV, KJV). Our passions and desires of our human nature were "put to death" when we aligned ourselves with Christ Jesus (see Galatians 5:24) but these strong feelings can resurrect themselves from time to time presenting us with challenges. But—and this is very important—because we belong to Christ, we can make choices; we can resist their power; we can defeat sin. We don't have to be held hostage by strong feelings. The Holy Spirit can direct our lives.

The human nature of the believers in Galatia was still very much around. It was obvious in the way they fought over how people were put right with God. Each side wanted their own way so much their human nature was surfacing as jealousy, envy, anger, bitterness, and resentment. Instead of letting this fighting go on and on, Paul said they should "Let the Spirit direct" (Galatians 5:16). I believe this is what we need to do with many of the emotional challenges we encounter. The question, though, is how? How do we let the Holy Spirit direct? Here are some things I've found helpful as I moved ahead after figuring out what was causing my "pangs of jealousy" and setting goals for the future.

Engage the will. The Holy Spirit's power is available to help us, but he is not going to overpower us and make us do things. As Kenneth S. Wuest writes in his word study on Galatians in the Greek New Testament, "The Holy Spirit is not a perpetual motion machine which operates automatically in the life of the believer. He is a divine Person waiting to be depended upon for his ministry and expecting the [believer] to cooperate with him."[1] Why wouldn't a person want to cooperate with the Spirit? Why wouldn't a Christian want to gain control of their feelings and do what is right? There's something comforting about our unrighteous feelings. It can feel good to tell ourselves just how unfair life is, how we never get any breaks, and how others make our life miserable. In our minds, we see ourselves as justified in feeling the way we do. *If no one else is going to pat us on the back, we'll do it ourselves.* We resist letting go of those feelings, and we are also fearful of what we might need to do if the Spirit leads. We might have to admit guilt, repent, or take action, such as separating from a group that feeds our resentment or making restitution to someone our jealousy or envy hurt in some way.

This is where *wanting* in a good sense matters. The Holy Spirit is near, ready to help, but he needs us to want his help for it to happen. He doesn't force himself on us.

Listen for the Spirit's voice. God's Spirit speaks to believers. He proclaims what's right, he convicts, he reassures, and he urges us to be faithful to do what God wants. We must develop a consciousness that hears him speak and a sensitivity for recognizing his voice. Other voices speak to us, too, but what the Holy Spirit says will be in line with Jesus, his nature, how he lived, and what he taught. Where we listen can also help us in our ability to hear. To hear the Holy Spirit speak may require time apart from others or from our many duties where we can listen without being distracted.

Make the right choice. "The will of the person has been liberated from the enslavement to sin which it experienced before salvation, and is free now to choose the right and refuse the wrong ... Thus the choice lies with the believer as to whether he is going to yield to the Holy Spirit or obey the evil nature. The Spirit is always there to give him victory over that nature as the [believer] says a point-blank NO to sin and at the same time trusts the Spirit to give him victory over it."[2] This is crucial. If we want a life directed by the Spirit, we must say "no" to what our sinful nature tempts us to do and do what God wants us to do.

Need to act. When "we live by the Spirit," we "keep in step with the Spirit." (Galatians 5:25 NIV). We conduct ourselves or order our behavior to match what the Spirit says is right and appropriate. We do not consistently and repeatedly engage in jealousy, envy, and coveting. We act in faith and trust God's Spirit to give us victory.

So when Paul says, "Let the Spirit direct your lives" (Galatians 5:16), he was urging believers not to let their human nature win. The power of sin has been broken; we don't have to give in to fleshly desires. We have the Spirit's strength to resist and not obey the urgings of our sinful nature. If we don't, the consequences could be dire. Paul warned, "If you bite and devour each other, watch out or you will be destroyed by each other" (Galatians 5:15 NIV). No wonder Paul went on to say, "You should each judge your own conduct. If it is good, then you can be proud of what you yourself have done, without having to compare it with what someone else has done" (Galatians 6:4). Here's a place where I tripped up as I moved forward in life.

Caught by Comparison

Once I discovered what was behind my "pangs of jealousy" and determined a future direction for my life, I set goals for myself and worked to meet them. This thrust me into a competitive environment. I'm not a competitive person by nature, so I sometimes reacted by being critical of some of the competition. One fellow writer in particular bothered me. She and I wrote on the same topic. As I read her postings on the internet, I thought my interpretation was better. The way I saw it, she didn't really "get it," and yet she received more acclaim and sold more books. Not fair!

One day she posted something that involved statistics—stats I was sure were wrong. Without checking, I responded in her comments section and tactfully corrected her. I did it nicely, but to me it spelled victory. While I didn't use the word, or even acknowledge it happening, I had one-upped her, and it felt good.

Later that morning, I had to make a trip from our rural home outside St. Louis into the city. As I drove, I delighted in what I had done. I replayed the scene over and over in my mind, and as I did, I actually said to myself, "Oh, this is so much fun." It's hard to imagine a born again, spirit-filled Christian, someone who knew better, saying something like this, but I did. I said it out loud, and I said it several times, smiling broadly as I did so. Then as the traffic picked up as I neared St. Louis, I stopped replaying the incident and focused on driving. Quiet followed. That's when I heard God's Spirit speak. He said, "Brenda, she's a fellow Christian. She's serving the Lord. She's a woman of influence. She's ministering in the name of Jesus, and you are feeling smug because you showed her to be wrong. Shame on you."

"Oh, my gosh," I said, "I'm jealous of her." In my times of being critical of her, I never called it jealousy, never thought of it as jealousy, but it was. Now that I knew it, I had to acknowledge it.

Now that was the work of the Holy Spirit. I heard him speak, convicting me of my guilt! I realized I shouldn't be judging her; I should be judging myself. Fortunately, I had grown enough through Bible study to know I needed to stop this jealousy immediately, and I did. There alone in the car, I confessed my jealousy out loud and asked God to forgive me. I said, "God, I've sinned. Please forgive me. Help me to do better." I repeated my prayer until my heart felt cleansed and renewed.

When I got home, it occurred to me maybe I ought to recheck those stats I had quoted. When I did, I realized I had misinterpreted them. I was wrong—not the author I was criticizing. Now that produced some humility in me! Not the fruit I was aiming for, but certainly one I needed.

Jealousy, envy, and coveting are feelings that are always going to be challenging. While we can improve and reduce the number of occurrences, we can never get to the point of saying *I will never be jealous*, or *in no way will I ever be envious*, or *you won't find me coveting something someone else has*. That's why we need to take Paul's advice and let the Spirit direct. We need to engage our will, listen for his voice, make the right choice, and take action. And the good news is, if we do this, we don't have to do this alone. He's always there to help us along the way.

Questions for Growth (Galatians 5:13–5:26):

1. What is the relationship between belief and behavior?
2. Since we are justified by faith, what is wrong with occasionally indulging our sinful nature?
3. If we are made alive by the Spirit, why do we still struggle with sin?
4. What Christian groups have you observed that divide into sides where jealousy and envy are present?
5. Which spiritual fruit is the Holy Spirit developing within you?
6. How can a Christian cause the fruit to grow in her life? What is the role of the Holy Spirit in this growth?
7. What results from following the Spirit's leadership?
8. How can you more effectively follow the Spirit's leadership?
9. Can you describe the fruit of the Spirit you possess without comparing it to the fruit others have?
10. Do all believers grow at the same rate in being led by the Spirit? What makes a difference in the rate of their growth?
11. How might a Christian deceive herself about following the Holy Spirit or about the fruit she has received in her life? How might this deception shape the fellowship she has with other believers?

CHAPTER 16—PAUL AND THE CORINTHIANS: WALK IN LOVE

If you had a physical ailment that repeated itself from time to time, wouldn't you start thinking about whether you could do something about it? Possibly make some kind of change in your lifestyle to see if it would help? For example, if you were experiencing repeated episodes of physical heartburn, you would look for solutions, wouldn't you? You would probably start by thinking about possible causes. Could it be spicy food? Greasy food? Too much caffeine? Eating too much at one time? Clothing too tight? Too much time sitting in a recliner? When you figure it out and make some changes, your reward will be fewer episodes of discomfort and a smoother life. Would an analysis like this be helpful for spiritual heartburn? Is there a better way to live that would reduce the number of episodes?

This is an important consideration because we will always have interactions or circumstances that spark jealousy, envy, or coveting unless we become hermits or recluses. We live in families, we work with people, we are a part of a body of believers, we deal with the public, we have friends—and sometimes an enemy or two. It's an atmosphere filled with comparison and competition; consequently, heart disruptions are certain to occur as we walk through life. We fret and stew as we deal with each one. Wouldn't it be better if we developed a lifestyle or a mindset that would help us have a smoother life? No, we can't eliminate the people in our lives. But is there something we can do so we won't experience so much spiritual heartburn? Something that would make life more pleasant?

I believe there is. It's what the apostle Paul called "a more excellent way" (1 Corinthians 12:31 KJV). He wrote about this "way" in a letter to a group of people who lived in an environment of jealousy and quarreling (see 1 Corinthians 3:3).

Chaos in Corinth

Various parties had formed among the Corinthian Christians. Some of them were devoted to Paul; others sided with Apollos, an eloquent teacher. Still others were devoted to the apostle Peter, and then there was another group whose members said, "We follow Christ!" They set themselves up above their Christian brothers and sisters as the really righteous group. You can imagine how that rankled the others. *Who do they think they are? God's gift to humanity?*

Other prickly matters bothering the Corinthian Christians were sexual immorality, lawsuits, and arguments. They also argued over whether to be single or married was better, whether women could minister in the church, the proper way to observe the Lord's Supper, and which spiritual gifts were the best. Many of them desired the gifts that edified the individual rather than the whole group. In other words, they wanted the gifts that made them look good.

Wouldn't you agree this would be an irritating environment—one optimum for spiritual heartburn? It appears that way to me. Every time I read Paul's letter to the Corinthians, I find it hard to believe they had so many heart-disturbing problems. The chance of their having a better way to live appears hopeless to me, but it didn't appear that way to Paul. He pointed this problem-riddled, heart-disturbing church to "a more excellent way" to live (1 Corinthians 12:31 KJV).

The Way of Love

By love, Paul didn't mean that warm fuzzy feeling that makes you want to hold a baby or pick up a cute three-year-old and plant kisses on her forehead. It is not the heart fluttering you get when sexually attracted to someone (this kind, *eros* love, might increase your heartburn). It is not the love you feel toward your coffee cup friends, those you share your secrets with. Rather what Paul recommended to them—and to us—is disciplined love, an act of the will. It is *agapē* love. Paul didn't define exactly what agapē love is, but he did describe it.

> Love is patient and kind; it is not jealous or conceited or proud; love is not ill-mannered or selfish or irritable; love does not keep a record of wrongs; love is not happy with evil, but is happy with the truth. Love never gives up; and its faith, hope, and patience never fail. (1 Corinthians 13:4–7)

To those of us who experience feelings of jealousy, envy, coveting, and resentment, Paul's remedy may seem almost impossible to apply. *The goal is too lofty. Why try*? Neither does he give any kind of specific guidance for how to love in his description. How can we follow a prescription if we don't have directions? I do best when I have guidelines, and as I studied Paul's description of what agapē love is and what it isn't, I found some. Over time, these guidelines have enabled me to experience less heartburn, and they continue to do so as I move forward in life

Be patient and kind: (1 Corinthians 13:4). When a jealous flash occurs or you're turning green with envy, don't be quick to jump to conclusions about what this might mean in your life or what the consequences might be. Rather, withhold judgment of yourself and of the other person (or persons) causing your heartburn. Show an interest in what others are doing. Offer to become involved in what they are planning. Help them reach their goals. As you do, your perspective will change. Your jealousy will fade, and envy will wind itself down. This is much better than being "conceited or proud" about your own projects and accomplishments (13:4)—an approach that will not help your heartburn. Instead it will likely make it worse.

Practice good manner: "Love is not ill-mannered or selfish or irritable" (1 Corinthians 13:5), so respecting each other and each other's property or possessions is important. The result makes for a more pleasant environment for all concerned.

To act without consideration of proper social behavior is to disrespect others. Little things count a lot in the home, at church, and at work to keep things harmonious, whereas being ill mannered stirs up trouble that is hard to forget. It is better to be mannerly.

- If she does something worthy of congratulations, congratulate her.
- Do you like your sister's new car or house? If so, tell her not begrudgingly, but pleasantly. "What a good choice you made!"
- Did your work partner do a good job on the sales presentation? Instead of wishing you could do as well—or better—commend your partner on a job well done.

Don't wait until you feel like being gracious. Express what the occasion calls for and you will start experiencing a change in how you feel. As pastor Andy Stanley says, "It's much easier to behave your way into a new way of thinking than to think your way into a new way of behavior."[1]

Don't keep a record of wrongs (1 Corinthians 13:5). When you are jealous or envious, it is tempting to start keeping a tally. You build up a score card of resentments such as she always gets there first, she always gets the easy assignments, he never has to hustle, and his group has more resources to work with than ours does. These incidents stack up in your mind. It's like you have a mental journal or ledger where you record offenses that sustain your heartburn. Never mind these offenses are not deliberately aimed at you, but you list them as if they are. This, though, is not characteristic of agapē love. It does not keep a record of wrongs.

Don't delight in evil (1 Corinthians 13:6 NIV). In other words, don't be happy with evil. What if that person you're jealous or envious of starts experiencing difficulties? Some of her projects fail? She gets in trouble? Stumbles and falls? Offends someone and is fired? You might delight in evil by saying "it's about time" or chuckle to yourself as you are secretly glad. You relish hearing derogatory remarks about her and are happy when you see troubling things happen to her. Agapē love, though, refuses to find pleasure in negative reports about other people. Instead, it believes the best of every person.

Rejoice with the truth (1 Corinthians 13:6 NIV) or be "happy with the truth" (1 Corinthians 13:6). When we are jealous, envious, covetous, or resentful, we may have a very narrow way of looking at things, seeing incidents from our perspective only. We may fail to see there's something greater, perhaps bigger, taking place.

This is what happened to the elder brother in Jesus's story about the prodigal son (Luke 15:11–32). The younger son, the prodigal, asked for his inheritance, got it, and took off. He spent his inheritance foolishly in another country. The elder brother stayed home and was a good son.

When the prodigal son returned home, the father was ecstatic. He held a big celebration. As the gaiety got underway, the older brother became angry and refused to join in the family festivities.

He said to his father, “Look, all these years I have worked for you like a slave, and I have never disobeyed your orders. What have you given me? Not even a goat for me to have a feast with my friends! But this son of yours wasted all your property on prostitutes, and when he comes back home, you kill the prize calf for him!” (Luke 15:29–30).

Sounds like he had a right to be angry, doesn’t it? He had been so good when the brother was faulty; it didn’t seem fair. The father didn’t respond with “I’ll try to make it up to you” or “I can see things from your perspective, I’ll throw you a party.” Instead he said, “My son ... you are always here with me, and everything I have is yours. But we had to celebrate and be happy, because your brother was dead, but now he is alive; he was lost, but now he has been found.” (Luke 15:31–32).

There was something greater going on here, something beyond fairness and equal treatment. A family was reunited. A lost son had returned home.

Agapē love gets the bigger picture; it recognizes that sometimes in a situation we’re regarding as unfair or unreasonable, a greater principle may need to be considered. This is why John the Baptist didn’t get jealous when his disciples did. To John, it wasn’t about greater crowds versus lesser crowds. It was about a mighty work of God taking place.

These are some helpful guidelines that I found in Paul’s description of agapē love. You may see other things because there are numerous ways to love inherent in this passage or even outside of this passage. The New Testament is full of references to agapē love.

- Paul also encouraged the Galatians, whose situation we considered in the last chapter, to love instead of fighting and quarreling. Paul, who considered keeping God’s commandments very important, said all God's commandments could be "summed up in one commandment: 'Love your neighbor as you love yourself'" (Galatians 5:14).

- James, an apostle, encouraged people who were fighting, quarreling, and coveting to love instead (see James 4:1–3). He said, "You will be doing the right thing if you obey the law of the Kingdom, which is found in the scripture ... 'Love your neighbor as you love yourself'" (James 2:8).
- Jesus said on more than one occasion we should love our neighbor as we love ourselves (see Matthew 22:39, Mark 12:31, and Luke 10:27b). It was a command he gave his followers: "Love one another. As I have loved you, so you must love one another" (John 13:34).

Consequently, I'm convinced practicing agapē love is the right thing to do when we are tempted to be jealous, envious, covetous, or resentful. There's just too much biblical evidence to believe otherwise, so when a vulnerable moment comes along, I don't have to debate about what I should do. There's no wasting energy trying to decide what's best. No vacillating back and forth. This is not to say actually doing it is easy. When it is a matter of discipline involving an act of the will, it makes it harder to practice than when we are moved by feelings. But here's what I've found: when I step forward in obedience, whether I feel like doing it or not, God responds and helps me follow through. His Spirit comes along and assists me.

When we believe what Jesus said and what Paul and James encouraged and we step forward in obedience, we will find ourselves mellowing. The jealousy we were feeling winds itself down and disappears. The item we were coveting so furiously no longer seems so important. The envy dominating our thoughts stops swirling around in our heads. The resentment we want to hold on to fades.

I've experienced this change in feeling time and time again when practicing agapē love. This is not to say I do it perfectly or respond appropriately every time, but it is to say I'm sold on a prescription that works for reducing spiritual heartburn. That's why I'm going to continue to choose to love when I'm tempted to be jealous, envious, covetous, or resentful. I'm going to walk in love. Are you?

QUESTIONS FOR GROWTH (1 CORINTHIANS 13):

1. Why are spiritual gifts useless without love (13:1–3)?
2. What are some characteristics of agapē love (13:4–7)? Of these characteristics, which one were you most surprised by? Which one do you need most to work on in your life?
3. Why might a person hesitate in putting agapē love into action?
4. What are some irritating challenges that make life difficult within families? Within a church? At work?
5. How long should a person be willing to practice living a "more excellent way" (1 Corinthians 13:7 KJV)?
6. What contrasts does Paul make in 1 Corinthians 13:8–12?
7. Why is love greater than faith and hope (1 Corinthians 13:13)?
8. Make a list of the positive qualities of agapē love in 1 Corinthians 13:4–7. Which one of these positive qualities is the most difficult for you to practice?
9. Make a list of the negative characteristics of agapē love in 1 Corinthians 13:4–7. Which one of these qualities are you most susceptible to committing?

CONCLUSION—A HEART AT PEACE

Remember how as a child you were interested in growth? You'd back up against another child, maybe a sibling or a friend, and say, "Look at us, Mom. Who's the tallest?" It was important to know. Growth mattered.

Or maybe you put markings on the wall like the children who lived in my house at one time. When we moved in, we spotted markings on a basement door frame: horizontal lines, dates, and initials. *Ah,* I thought, *children have lived here*. The markings showed their physical growth through the years. Eventually, the marks ceased; the children had reached their full physical height. They had become adults.

We don't do markings on the wall for adults. We don't back up to our friends and ask someone to measure who is tallest. We do, though, grow; that is, if we want to. We can grow just as Jesus grew. He increased in wisdom, in stature, and in favor with God and man (see Luke 2:52 KJV).

Growing Wiser

In this book, we had the opportunity to increase our knowledge by looking at various biblical characters. We learned about the power of *wanting*, times in which we are vulnerable, the characteristics of jealousy, envy, and coveting, and the consequences of not dealing with these emotions. Knowledge isn't the same as wisdom, but you can't have wisdom without some knowledge.

We started with Eve. Her heart was disturbed by *wanting*. Her experience shows us how what we *see* influences what we *want*, particularly as it relates to the senses, to what is attractive, and to one-upmanship.

Cain alerted us to the power of comparative eyes. As we compare, we become dissatisfied with who we are and what we have. Comparison is often present in episodes of jealousy, envy, and coveting. It affected Sarah as she compared her sons at play and changed her mind about what she *wanted*.

Many families are beset with tensions and conflicts that lead siblings to be envious or jealous of each other. The hearts of Joseph's brothers were disturbed for years as a result of being jealous. Aaron and Miriam criticized their brother Moses because they weren't getting any recognition for their contributions.

The experiences of Saul, David, Ahab, and Achan remind us that even when we have much we still want more. Sometimes we want something so much that we go against our values, forget reason, and break God's commandments.

Our emotions get tangled in our hearts by getting angry over the prosperity or success of others such as Asaph's and Daniel's critics did.

Our hearts become fertile ground for growing jealousy and envy when we start thinking in terms of "my group" and "your group" as the disciples of John the Baptist did and the Jews who were jealous of Jesus and of Paul.

As troubling as jealousy, envy, and coveting are, various biblical characters showed us how to deal with these feelings. Asaph's example taught us about the power of sanctuary. John the Baptist's experience suggested letting Jesus increase while we decrease. From Simon Magus, we saw the need for repentance, prayer, and confession, and from Paul, we learned numerous ways to let the Spirit direct our lives and to walk in love.

These experiences raised our awareness of these emotions in our lives, taught us their characteristics and alerted us to the damage they can do to hearts and to relationships. As we gained this knowledge, our wisdom developed as we worked on the growth questions and applied what we learn. It's not really wisdom unless it helps us make sense of life and make decisions. We think, we recall, we meditate, and we act. Even if we sometimes fail, we can still grow in wisdom. There's always something to learn from our experiences.

Our Stature

As adults we stop growing in height, although some of us lose height as we age. But stature as a description doesn't always mean physical height. Stature can also mean a quality or status gained by growth, development, or achievement. Or it could mean that you are worthy of esteem or recognition. In other words, you stand out among all the others in your field.

Stature could also be how you present yourself to others. Maybe you've noticed the way people who are jealous or envious sometimes carry themselves: shoulders bent forward, disgruntled look, poor posture, face frowning. When you apply what you have learned, really take in the message, your countenance changes. You stand straighter, hold your shoulders back, and breathe easier.

We don't have to look to our right or our left to see what others are doing and try to compete with them. We know who we are. We don't get sucked into continually comparing ourselves with others or being overly competitive. We can stand tall and be our own person.

In Favor with God

Being in favor with God doesn't mean God is partial—that he is going to give you special favors because you completed a Bible study. God loves everyone. To be in his "favor" means having an open relationship, nothing standing in the way of communicating with him. You feel blessed, as if a light is shining on your path. You can see more clearly. My vision was cloudy because I had spiritual heartburn. There was something within keeping me from being in favor with God. I thought it was the fleeting feelings of jealousy occurring in my life. But as I gained knowledge and grew wiser, I became more reflective. That's when I discovered my real problem was disappointment in God. Something was indeed affecting our relationship. The experiences of Asaph and John the Baptist helped me figure this out and guided me on what to do about it. Then I was in his favor once again, and that's where I want to stay. I want to see clearly and be aware of light shining on the path I'm walking.

This realization was important to me because as I explained in the book, I am a woman who craves inner peace. This is still true. When my relationship with God isn't what it could be, my heart is disturbed. Discovering what was behind my "pangs of jealousy" and improving my relationship with God, I gained a heart at peace that gave life to my midlife bones and beyond. I was able to move on with joy and anticipation of what's next, and I want to keep it that way. That's why I watch over my "heart with all vigilance, for from it flow the springs of life" (Proverbs 4:23 NRSV).

In Favor with Man

How much of your life is taken up with relationships? Families. Children. Coworkers. Fellow church members. Small groups. Social groups. Teams. Never did we become more aware of our lives being intertwined with others than during the COVID-19 pandemic when we had to isolate ourselves and become individualists. We missed our relationships, and we realized how important they are to our well-being and to navigating life. But as our study showed us, there can also be friction involved when we become jealous, envious, or covetous, resulting in spiritual heartburn, just like these feelings can interfere with our relationship with God.

Now that we have studied the experiences of biblical characters, we are aware of some of the dynamics involved in relationships. We better understand why people act the way they do. At the same time, we can also be more analytical about our own lives. We're not afraid to look inward and ask, why do I feel this way? Or why do I react the way I sometimes do? What can I do about my feelings that are interfering with my relationships? This book gives us numerous tools for successfully dealing with feelings and creating harmonious relationships. It's up to us whether or not we use them, and we will if we want to be in favor with others.

Because I have grown in wisdom, in stature, and in my relationships with others and with God doesn't mean I will *never* be jealous again. I don't think there's any way to keep me from *never* being jealous—jealous flashes will occur. But here's the difference. I can recognize them, and I can do something about them. I don't wait around and let the emotion morph into something bigger or have a long-term influence. I have plenty of insight and strategies from the examples of the biblical characters to deal with heart issues.

How about you? Have you grown? As we measure ourselves to see how much we've grown, it is not to measure ourselves against others. We're no longer children. Rather measuring our growth means looking at *our* lives, where we've been and where we're going. It's seeing a difference, a before and an after. It can be a small amount of growth, a large amount, or somewhere in between, but still a change has taken place.

We can mark new growth on the timeline of our life. Our biblical exploration of jealousy, envy, coveting, and related emotions enables us to stand tall and be spiritually healthy because we're more appreciative of who we are and because we know how to clear up our inner space so our relationship with God can thrive. Keeping the lessons we learned in mind—and applying them—will serve us well in controlling our *wanting*, maintaining "a heart of peace," and giving "life to" our bodies for years to come (Proverbs 14:30a NIV).

ABOUT THE AUTHOR

Brenda Poinsett is a Christian communicator with a passion for learning and teaching. For fifteen years, she was an adjunct instructor at Oakland City University's Bedford, Indiana, campus. At midlife, she sensed a need to broaden her classroom. Building on the sturdy foundation of her formal education (BS, MRE), years of intense study, and wisdom gained from life experiences, Brenda speaks, leads Bible studies, counsels women's groups, and writes books.

Her strength as a speaker, teacher, and writer is her ability to share in a clear, easy-to-follow manner with lots of illustrations, applications, and guidelines. She's the author of over twenty books including *Wonder Women of the Bible*, *The Friendship Factor*, *When Saints Sing the Blues*, *Holiday Living* and *He Said What?! Jesus' Amazing Words to Women*.

These books give readers sources of wisdom for times of need as well as for times of joy.

Brenda and her husband Bob live near St. Louis, Missouri. They have three grown sons, one daughter-in-law and three grandchildren. You can learn more about Brenda or contact her for speaking through her website www.BrendaPoinsett.com.

ENDNOTES

Chapter 1

1. E. Stanley Jones, *The Way: 362 Adventures in Daily Living* (Nashville: Abington Press, 1946), page 244.

2. Herschel H. Hobbs, *Studying Adult Life and Work Lessons*, April May June 1978, page 28.

Chapter 2

1. Daniel Goleman, *Emotional Intelligence* (New York: Bantam Books, 1998), page 290.

Chapter 3

1. The New International Version of the Bible says: "But Sarah saw that the son whom Hagar the Egyptian had borne to Abraham was mocking" (Genesis 21:9). The New King James Version says they were scoffing. I'm more inclined to agree with GNB and NRSV translations. Each says the boys were playing.

Chapter 4

1. The King James Version uses "envied" to describe what the brothers felt (see Genesis 37:11). The New Revised Standard edition, the New English Bible and The Good News Bible say, "jealous."

Chapter 5

1. For more on this topic see Elizabeth Bernstein's article, "Why Being Kind Helps You, Too—Especially Now," in the August 12, 2020 edition of *The Wall Street Journal*, page A12.

2. Peter Toohey, *Jealousy* (New Haven, Connecticut: Yale University Press, 2014), page 44.

3. Eugene H. Peterson, *The Message: The New Testament, Psalms, and Proverbs* (Colorado Springs, Colorado: Navpress, 1993, 1994, and 1995), page 402.

Chapter 6

1. Not her real name.

Chapter 7

1. I make a case for this in my book, *When Saints Sing the Blues: Understanding Depression through the Lives of Job, Naomi, Paul, and Others* (Grand Rapids, Michigan: Baker Books, 2006).

2. Peter Toohey, *Jealousy* (New Haven, Connecticut: Yale University Press, 2014, page 3.

Chapter 9

1. Joseph Epstein, *Envy* (The New York Public Library: Oxford University Press, 2003), page 4.

2. *Ibid.*, page 57.

Chapter 10

1. Alice Fryling, *Reshaping a Jealous Heart* (Downers Grove, Illinois: InterVarsity Press, 1994), page 37.

Chapter 12

1. Christians see Jesus's death as the plan and purpose of God being carried out, and rightly so, but the actions of the chief priests and Pharisees also show us the extreme of what can happen when jealousy and fear become intertwined.

2. This advice also appears in Matthew 5:43–44.

Chapter 13

1. Not her real name.

2. William Barclay, *The Gospel of John, Volume 1, The Daily Study Bible* (Edinburgh, Scotland: The Saint Andrew Press, 3rd edition, 1964), page 132.

3. Eugene Peterson, *The Message: The New Testament, Psalms and Proverbs (Colorado Springs, Colorado: Navpress, 1993, 1994, and 1995*), page 193.

4. Reference to something Jeremiah said in 20:9.

Chapter 14

1. R. T. Kendall, *Jealousy: The Sin No One Talks About: How to Overcome Envy & Live a Life of Freedom* (Lake Mary, Florida: Charisma House, 2010), page 126.

2. Carey Nieuwhof, *Didn't See It Coming* (Colorado Springs, Colorado: WaterBrook, 2018), page 139.

Chapter 15

1. Kenneth S. Wuest, *Wuest's Word Studies: Galatians in the Greek New Testament for the English Reader* (Grand Rapids, Michigan: Wm. B. Eerdmans Publishing Company, 1944), page 154.

2. *Ibid.*

Chapter 16

1. Andy Stanley, *It Came From Within!: The Terrifying Truth of What Lurks in the Heart* (Sisters, Oregon: Multnomah Publishers, 2006), page 194.

BIBLIOGRAPHY

Ashcraft, Morris. Genesis: Foundations for Faith. *Advanced Bible Study*, Volume 8, Number 3 (April, May, June 1978).

Barclay, William. *The Gospel of John, Volume I, The Daily Study Bible*. Edinburgh, Scotland: The Saint Andrew Press, 3rd edition, 1964.

Beecher, Marguerite and Willard. *The Mark of Cain: An Anatomy of Jealousy*. New York: Harper and Row, 1971.

Braithwaite, Althea. *Exploring Emotions: Feeling Jealous*. Milwaukee, Wisconsin: Gareth Stevens Publishing, 1998.

Dormen, Lesley. "Taming Envy," *Good Housekeeping*, January 2010, pages 103-104,108.

Epstein, Joseph. *Envy*. The New York Public Library: Oxford University Press, 2003.

Friday, Nancy. *Jealousy*. New York: William Morrow and Company, Inc., 1985.

Fryling, Alice. *Reshaping a Jealous Heart*. Downers Gove, Illinois: InterVarsity Press, 1994.

Goleman, Daniel. *Emotional Intelligence*. New York: Bantam Books, 1998.

Hauck, Paul A. *Overcoming Jealousy and Possessiveness*. Philadelphia: The Westminister /John Knox Press, 1981.

Hobbs, Herschel H. *Studying Adult Life and Work Lessons*, April, May, June 1978.

Jones, E. Stanley. *The Way: 364 Adventures in Daily Living*. Nashville: Abingdon Press, 1946.

Kendall, R. T. *Jealousy: The Sin No One Talks About: How to Overcome Envy & Live a Life of Freedom*. Lake Mary, Florida: Charisma House, 2010.

Kirshenbaum, Mira. *The Emotional Energy Factor: The Secrets High-Energy People Use to Beat Emotional Fatigue*. New York, NY: A Delta Book published by Delacorte Press, 2004.

Leahy, Robert L. *The Jealousy Cure: Learn to Trust, Overcome Possessiveness & Save Your Relationship*. Oakland, California: New Harbinger Publications, Inc., 2018.

Lockyer, Herbert. *All the Women of the Bible*. Grand Rapids, Michigan: Zondervan Publishing House, no copyright date listed.

Lutzer, Erwin W. *Failure: The Back Door to Success*. Chicago, Illinois: Moody Press, 1975.

Nieuwhof, Carey. *Didn't See It Coming*. Colorado Springs, Colorado: Waterbrook, 2018.

Smedes, Lewis B. *Love Within Limits*. Grand Rapids, Michigan: William B. Eerdmans Publishing Company, 1978.

Stanley, Andy. *It Came From Within*!: *The Terrifying Truth of What Lurks in the Heart*. Sisters, Oregon: Multnomah Publishers, 2006.

Telushkin, Rabbi Joseph. *Biblical Literacy: The Most Important People, Events, and Ideas of the Hebrew Bible*. New York: William Morrow and Company, Inc., 1997.

Toohey, Peter. *Jealousy*. New Haven, Connecticut: Yale University Press, 2014.

Wuest, Kenneth S. *Wuest's Word Studies: Galatians in the Greek New Testament for the English Reader*. Grand Rapids, Michigan: Wm. B. Eerdmans Publishing Company, 1944.

Made in USA - North Chelmsford, MA
1276133_9781649493859
09.23.2021 1551